*ANGNA ENTERS: ON MIME*

# *ANGNA ENTERS*

## *on Mime*

WITH DRAWINGS BY THE AUTHOR

*WESLEYAN UNIVERSITY PRESS*

MIDDLETOWN, CONNECTICUT

ISBN 0-8195-6056-1
Library of Congress Catalog Card Number: 65-21130
Manufactured in the United States of America
First paperback edition, 1978

FOR RALPH PENDLETON

# Contents

DRAWINGS

*ANGNA ENTERS: ON MIME*

## Overture

Mimesis is the representation of reality by means of actions, with or without words. It is that form of theatre in which the actor-as-dramatist delineates characters *of his own creation*.

The mime is not an imitator. He enlarges, emphasizes, particularizes, comments on the character he portrays. It is as though images in the creator's memory, or flashes of vision, acting as catalytic agents, suddenly decide to have a being of their own. Then the creator-as-performer has to release these images to take their own shape, using whatever theatre forms are necessary to their realization.

In that sense, these images-become-characters are symbols: symbols natural to the reality of performer and audience; characters who are our brothers and sisters in whatever time, place, or theme — in the sense, say, that Madame Bovary is a character created by Flaubert and is also an individual unto herself, part of our collective imagination.

In mime, communication with the outside world is made by means of gesture-symbols.

These symbols are the result of the crystallization of experiences all men and women are heir to. They are a kind of semaphoric code — gesture, smile, glance, reflective thought, or physical action — by which we understand one another.

Mime is the oldest and the youngest means of dramatic expression, and the most generally universal. It lends itself in the theatre to every form, yet it retains its own form.

It is an elusive art, as its expression is entirely dependent on the imagination of the performer in the re-creation of his view of the character each time he performs.

Mime — or pantomime — is not the one best means of theatre expression. It is best only for that for which there are no words or for which too many words would be required.

### The Mime and the Poet

The mime and the poet have this in common — the image. The mime consolidates his image through nuances of expression, for which words are at most symbols; the poet transmits his image in the association of words in composition.

The viewers of the mime capture his meaning within the elasticity of their own understanding, just as the hearers of the poet relate each image to individual experience.

There are nuances of human exchange in which mime is the most direct medium of communication, and there are word images which mime can never approximate. The mime and the poet additionally have this in common: their *purpose,* and its relationship to music.

The *meter* of the mime to his image is as composed as that of a poet to his.

### Past and Present

Mime is a many-sided medium, and what I give here is but one mime's approach to that medium. My approach is that in mime one can present images of women and men in characteristic personal moments of their being in contrapuntal relation to a particular moment in time, and at the same time crystallize a kind of similarity in human behavior down through the ages. As I wrote some years ago, my purpose is:

4

To give personal form to a general experience.

To make the present visible by using it to telescope what in the past was then present. It was necessary to see the past through the present, for we see what has been in terms of our own being in the present.

Thus the past would emerge as present, disclosing the essential continuity of the nature of man. The modes, manners, and rhythms were merely masks, beneath which were the old familiar universal faces of man and woman.

A mode or manner can be concrete as a stone, which when dropped in the sea of human behavior makes a whirlpool in which is swallowed a whole generation and, in time, a civilization.

Yet there always is a thread with that past. In painting it is "the classic line" which emerges as "modern." And in modes and manners it is always human behavior which emerges as contemporary. Of course every age considered itself modern — even when it didn't think about it.

Topical telescoping of the past in terms of the present was characteristic of the Greek dramatists when they retold the sacred myths in terms of their own time. Very faint was the allegory to the political tyrannies, social foibles, and idiocies of their own day.

Using a past period as a mirror one might succeed in seeing — in showing — one's own time. *

### The Classic Line
(*Journal note — 8th June, 1933*)

Am tormented by elusive abstraction known as the "classic line." What is it? No matter how much one reads about it, or sees it, or recognizes it in others' achievements, it remains the unknown so far as one's own work is concerned. It is the true and perfect and variable line of life no matter how it is employed. One must find it for oneself like a child learning to walk. Applying it literally to a drawing one discovers that if one had a perfect photographic eye and could draw a figure exactly as though one had measured it, or placed a string around the form of the body, that it inevitably would be a dull lifeless drawing. The important thing is not the exact outline, but a line which suggests the fullnesses, thinnesses, the forms and solids which make each figure itself. All this theorizing is a release — a kind of cutting away of "tradition" — to one's instinctive approach.*

## The Take-Off

"Beware, oh painter, when theory outstrips performance."

— *Leonardo da Vinci*

The artist-as-artisan seeks to discover through experimentation how to most effectively adapt the tools of his craft toward the realization of his over-all purpose. A technique evolves gradually and partly unconsciously. Eventually it is instrumental in forming what is called the artist's "recognizable style." It is the function of technique to make a work of art appear the inevitable consummation of an idea or emotion without drawing primary attention to itself.

During many years of performing the form of mime associated with me, I was often questioned on my method of working. I answered that my approach is to permit any idea free-

---

* From *First Person Plural*, by Angna Enters, with illustrations by the author. Copyright © 1937, 1965 by Angna Enters. New York, Stackpole Sons, 1937.

6

dom to proscribe its own form. My interrogators were never satisfied with this — they seemed to feel that I had some secret formula that I was unwilling to reveal. The truth was that since I worked alone it never occurred to me to theorize on the subject, as it was unnecessary to explain to myself my way of working.

Around 1958 I was invited to conduct a class of players in the study of mime in relation to acting. I refused the invitation, as it was my conviction that the creative aspect of mime could not be taught, and I saw no way of reducing my free-form method into a communicable format.

The director of this dramatic academy did not accept my rejection of the invitation. After several years of continual attempts to persuade me that it was my "duty" not to withhold from young players what I had learned in performance, I consented to try teaching for one term.

What made me decide to attempt what seemed to me the impossible was that for some years I had had to forego developing ideas for extensions in mime beyond what I could do as a solo performer. Here, I thought, is a chance to experiment. I was assured that the group selected to work with me would not require a course in physical exercises, as they had all had training in movement, and that they would be interested in "anything" I had to tell them. I asked that the group be limited to eight so that each would have ample opportunity for individual attention.

Having committed myself, I pondered how to begin and concluded that before making plans it would be best to wait until I met the students and discovered their needs.

I embarked on the adventure as a Candide, unsuspecting of the hazards to be encountered. The LOG which follows is a record of this experience. It is interspersed with ASIDES, in which

7

I recount some of the experiences and thoughts that played a part in the evolution of my particular form of theatre.

## Log: First Session

Went prepared with nothing but a dual feeling of exhilaration and queasiness to face the group for the first time. To my astonishment, there were twenty expectant faces staring at me instead of the more intimate circle I had expected. This required a rapid readjustment of perspective!

Explained that they must not expect a formula technique from me, as it would be my endeavor to help them develop their own inventive powers. This was greeted with a reassuring shout of approval, understandable when they confessed themselves weary of being presented with exercises difficult to apply to their individual needs.

The group proved to be heterogeneous in experience and purpose. Most are actors with varying degrees of professional or semiprofessional experience. Several are dancers, two wish to make solo mime their profession, and one is a young singer studying for opera. A. came to the group accompanied by a student-secretary, who was armed with a notebook, presumably to write down everything I had to say.

The moment had come to outline my approach to mime — which is, without set technical formula, to permit any idea, so far as possible, to dictate its own form. It is my aim to free the characters of my theatre from any trademark representative of my own personality.

Of course it is impossible for any human being to divorce his point of view from anything which he does, but I try not to deflect the audience from concentration on the character. That is, I try to conceal my own identity from the audience as much as possible. To this end, when considerable movement is

8

involved, I restrain any display of technical proficiencies. That is, I do not wish for an audience to ever marvel at *how* something is accomplished — only *what*, in relation to the character or idea performed.

I work simply. I become obsessed with an idea having to do with some aspect of human behavior, or with the aspect of an age. The figure who best symbolizes the idea knocks on the door of my consciousness, and I welcome it. Whether this idea or character will interest an audience is pure chance. While it is true that I may have doubts as to whether there will be audience interest, I *must* try to clarify, through mime, what is in my thoughts. I have never been so vain as to believe that an audience was less able to understand than I am. Experience has taught me that what is clear to me, given considered direction, can be communicated.

This introduction led to questions of specific moments in certain numbers in my theatre, particularly "Pavana — Sixteenth-Century" — the face, the movement, and the use of the large handkerchief.

Explained that the "Pavana," an early work which found a permanent place in my repertoire, was representative of a habit of doing variations on and exploring the many possibilities of a theme of ideas, much in the manner that a composer improvises on a melodic theme.

*Inception of the "Pavana"*

In this case, "Pavana" was the result of a series concerned with aspects of sixteenth- and seventeenth-century French court life.

In reading a memoir of those times, I had come upon an account of a ball where a *pavanne* had been danced, a dance so named from a particular step and flourish of the cape by the men, symbolic of a peacock. With this attractive image in mind, and with the aid of a woodcut illustration, I wondered how I, as a woman and as a single performer, could improvise on an extension of this theme so as to present an acceptable picture of an age.

In further readings, I came upon the fact that the dance had originated in Spain, which threw my curiosity toward that country. In this way I came to know the vast difference between the life of the women of the court in France and Spain, including their attitudes toward their religious observances.

I was already somewhat familiar with the paintings of the period and had been impressed by the brooding aspect of the Velasquez Infantas with their undershot Hapsburg lips.

"How would it be were I to make a composite picture of sixteenth-century Spain, using the *pavana* as a base and having it danced by an Infanta?" I asked myself.

This question clamored for resolution.

I have never been interested in mime as photographic reproduction of anything seen; which, of course, in the case of any abstract idea is impossible anyway. It is my attempt to let ideas evolve according to the vagaries of imagination, but based on my knowledge of the subject and the extent to which it can be communicated to others in mime.

This portrait of an Infanta was, then, to incorporate what I knew of that dance, her character, and the age and society in which she lived. A poetic abstraction.

In it I tried to portray her arrogance through the preening, peacock movements of her head and shoulders; her brooding nature by her Hapsburg face, in which I found that it was her mouth which, drawing down the muscles below her eyes, gave them their agonized contour — which could be used for malevolent expressions as well. (As a side note, I also became aware of the fact that it is the power of this muscle of which El Greco was aware in his painting of eyes.)

10

*Pavana Head*

The large handkerchief, then a new fashion, was used for dramatic accents, both in bringing out nuances of meaning and in the phrasing of movements.

The music, used as contrapuntal background, was a *pavana* of the period from the Escurial collection, although it required some adaptations for the piano for tonal fulfillment. To accent the mood, I chose an undercurrent of sound from a drum in a repetitive but not single beat, which recalled to me (though it was not the same) the muffled drums I had once heard, perhaps over the radio, in a funeral cortege.

This explanation of the inception of the "Pavana" I found had an unexpected subduing effect, because, it then occurred to me for the first time, they were accustomed to being directed in the performance of ready-made characters.

To lighten the atmosphere, asked for someone to perform, in mime, some idea which had to do with a few moments in the life of a person. Consternation! Then the girl who hopes to develop a solo form in mime took courage and gave a short number which had been too obviously based on my "Aphrodisiac — Green Hour" — a prostitute at a café defeated in pursuing her profession by a sudden rain. The player's conception was baldly naïve. Unfortunately, the discussion which followed dwelled on irrelevancies, and before we got to the real point, the time was up.

I think that the group is somewhat shaken at the prospect of confronting all the problems which lie ahead, although the meeting ended in a burst of applause, which I take to be a convention at dramatic academies.

## Log: Second Session

Proposed what seemed to me a practical plan for working: that since the majority of the group were actors interested in the

13

dramatic theatre, it might be advantageous to them and of equal value to all to invent a mime-play in which each would have a character to develop. It would give more opportunity than if the whole class were to work on the same character session after session, as in a play each one could observe the problems of the others, in addition to those of his own character.

This suggestion met with unanimous approval, especially when I told them that our aim would be to ready the play for public view.

Stipulated that the play was to be of their own invention, not mine, and asked for ideas.

What happened was this: The ideas offered stemmed entirely from their considerable knowledge of plays. The plays suggested were by Molière, Wilde, Chekhov, and Ibsen. I pointed out that these plays were primarily literary works and could not be easily translated into mime and still retain their nuances of meaning. Moreover, none provided a sufficient number of characters for all.

Then explained that I have a rigid rule in my own theatre never to become involved in a situation where lack of speech becomes evident. That when imaginary persons are present on my stage, I only listen and respond to what I hear by means of gesture or facial expression. I never caricature speech, but do only that for which words are not required. In reviewing in their memories what I do, they recognized that this was true.

They were interested but somewhat surprised when I also told them that my knowledge of "period" had not been gleaned from plays or stage conventions, but from the sources of history, from literature, or, for example, in some particulars, from such sources as the autobiographical writings of Saint-Simon (a stranger to them) and from painting. Painting in the sense that from it one learned one view of an age — that of its artists. As a specific example, I mentioned that it was a convention in archaic Greek sculpture to carve a woman holding the folds of a skirt across her body and in one hand. To me at least, it seems reasonable to assume that this was no

14

contrived effect of some artist, but was instead a stylized recognition of the fact that the women did actually hold their skirts thus to prevent them from flowing while walking.

The stylization of a natural gesture.

Thereupon someone suggested that we choose a classical Greek play, but I dissuaded them from the idea: the period was too remote for our immediate purpose, which was to focus on the details of human behavior possible to express in mime. That is, I did not wish them to have any remembrance of a classical play they had seen, but to start with something nearer in time.

A player mentioned that the film *La Ronde*, then being shown, afforded possibilities, as it had sufficient characters to accommodate the entire group. While I accepted this as a possibility, to my mind it contained two faults as regards our venture. First, it presented a ready-made scenario; and second, it was too episodic for a unified endeavor.

This talk did, however, recall another work, Schnitzler's novelette *Fraulein Else*, which would provide possibilities for extended improvisation. It also had the advantage of being just removed enough in time to supply a study of period, yet not so far that the group might not be able to recapture it through remembered tales of grandparents or parents. Rather than spend more time in search for a subject I suggested that we use this, and briefly outlined its possibilities, extemporizing as ideas occurred to me.

This suggestion was accepted largely because it released them from the obligation of presenting other ideas.

Roughly outlined, Schnitzler's story has to do with a young girl on holiday at a Baltic seaside resort. Her parents, in financial straits, telephone her to intercede for them for a loan from a rich acquaintance who is staying at the same hotel. The payment he exacts from her before he is willing to relieve her parents' financial burden she finds repugnant, and she seeks release in an overdose of veronal.

On this basis, and with additional side dramas to provide an ample part for everyone, we improvised a mime-play.

## Scene

To be enacted within the span from mid-afternoon into night without interruption. The setting, the terrace café of the hotel. Entrance to the hotel to the RIGHT. Off LEFT is a park, where a band concert takes place until sunset. The cyclorama is the sea, and between it and the café is a promenade.

Impatient to get down to work, in addition to Else and the man whom I called "the Industrialist," I invented characters who I thought might logically appear at any resort, and assigned these parts to the group. The dramatic relation of these new characters to the rest of the play was to evolve later, as ideas occurred to me. This process is the exact reverse of writing a play.

CAST

1 — Else
2 — The Industrialist
3 — Else's Aunt (has brought her and is an acquaintance of the Industrialist — who she hopes will be attracted to her niece)
4 — A Maid
5 — A Waiter
6 — A Tramp (this for a player interested in solo mime)
7 — A Woman of the World
8 — A Man of the World (her lover)
9 — A Young Man
10 — A Young Woman Tourist
11 — A Gigolo who is also a procurer
12 — A Prostitute, his friend
13 — A Poet

16

14 — A Middle-aged Man on a wedding anniversary holiday
15 — His Wife
16 — A Neurotic Young Woman who promenades alone
17–18 — Two young Girls of the town who promenade (the dancers)
19–20 — A Young Couple in love who promenade (least experienced)

We set our scene, luckily finding enough small tables and using the classroom folding chairs as café chairs. Our stage is small but adequate: 22 feet across and 16 deep.

In my eagerness to get started, and contrary to my resolution that everything would be the creation of the players, I assigned the tables according to my mental image. In the first rough blocking, the characters made their entrances as I dictated and took their places at the assigned tables or on the promenade.

When I first agreed to undertake this venture, the director of the school wished to limit the session to one hour, but I insisted on an hour and a half. It is already evident that my time proviso is a modest calculation.

I have a tendency to talk too extensively on any question that arises!

## Log: Third Session

Began with walk-through in order of entrances, some to take places at tables, with the purpose of becoming familiar with the time and space needed for this accomplishment.

Next asked for a run-through in which each would improvise on the character assigned.

This was unsuccessful, for either they had formed no view of their character; or they were too shy to improvise for fear of appearing absurd; or they were unable to translate thoughts

**17**

into action. Did not expect this contingency, since they had been voluble and not imperceptive in critical comments on the acting in plays running currently.

They were, I think, shaken at discovering the difficulty of performing, without words, characters that seemed simple enough when briefly outlined. How to resolve a general idea into definite form!

It therefore seemed advisable to work on one short segment in detail, with all observing. By this device they would learn how to approach their own parts.

I chose one scene which, because use of properties was involved, might be easiest as a starter. This was the first scene between the Industrialist and the Waiter.

### Premise

The Industrialist is a familiar patron of this resort hotel and his preferences are known to the Waiter, to whom he is a valued patron. As such, he is welcomed with the proper note of professional obsequiousness and given such special small attentions as the drawing out of his chair, an unnecessary quick wiping of the chair and table, the lighting of his cigar.

This accomplished, the Waiter looks at him inquiringly and receives a nod of assent. This is a sign for the Waiter to bring him his customary, special — let us say — Madeira.

The Waiter withdraws while the Industrialist relaxes and looks about casually to see who is present.

(Suggested that to fill in the interval of waiting, this may prove a good time for the Man and Woman of the World to enter and seat themselves at the table immediately UP-LEFT of that of the Industrialist.)

The Waiter now returns with a tray containing a bottle and glass, serves the wine, and leaves to take the order of the newcomers.

What happened was this: The Waiter performed the task too quickly and without any indication of the character as an individual.

18

Explained: In mime every moment must have dramatic purpose. It is not only *what* is done but *how* it is done that gives it meaning. In mime, the character portrayed has a dual identity. It is the embodiment of a recognizable universal type and is also an individual with behavior particular to him or her self.

In the case of waiters, one might say that they perform a kind of dance conditioned by their profession. Their movements are never jerky, and even when in haste they move easily, with a rather flat-footed glide-step, brought about by having to balance trays, their bodies twisting automatically to avoid collisions with chairs and tables. They bend slightly at the table and swing the tray or serving dish from the shoulder before lowering it with the elbow. This gesture is a habit acquired through performing their duties with the greatest ease, and it is often exaggerated by those who add a note of elegance to their service.

In this case, after setting down the tray, the Waiter should have shown the label to his client before uncorking the bottle. He might, then, before pouring it, have given the glass an extra polish, then partially filled the glass and watched its testing intently. The Industrialist ought to have taken a sip, allowed it to roll on his tongue, swallowed it, waited a second, and then nodded approval — a nod echoed by the Waiter, both smiling. The Waiter now would fill the glass, pick up his tray, the bottle upon it, and go to the table of the newcomers to receive their order.

In this entire short scene it is the individual exchange of thoughts between the characters which determines the timing.

In the handling of his implements, the hands of the Waiter must work with ease born of familiarity with his duty. His towel is not put on the table but is placed over his arm when not in use. The glass is lifted by the stem and the bottle by its cylinder, not by the neck. (Details obviously unknown by the player.)

Everything to be accomplished with the utmost economy of movement.

Spoke about the necessity of establishing an over-all mood for the play and suggested that it might be of value to them to read *Fraulein Else* and the short stories of Thomas Mann — not to get ideas for their characters (this they were to do on their own!) — but to get a sense of the aroma of the period.

Examination of the details of this short episode filled our entire time.

## *Log: Fourth Session*

It was apparent that working in unaccustomed silence was difficult for the group and made it impossible for them to sustain any feeling of unity, not only in the play as a whole, but in their separate parts.

To facilitate this, had brought in a record player and a recording of "The Emperor Waltz" as a sound stimulus, and this addition was met with whole-hearted approval.

Before the run-through, asked them to waltz about the studio floor to ingrain a feeling of the waltz rhythm, which seemed to provide a compatible background for our project. To my astonishment, they were all unfamiliar with the waltz, except for the several dancers, who related it to a step learned in ballet class. To the others, social dancing was confined to the current modes of Rock and Roll and its variations or the popular South American rhythms of the samba, the conga, etc. They soon grasped the step and rhythm and waltzed about freely, solo; but dancing with partners was not only confusing but also embarrassing, as the men and women were too timid to abandon themselves in each others' arms. Although they often speak of their readings in psychology, and although a number of them have undergone "analysis," these do not appear to have relieved their inhibitions; they still performed self-consciously. However, by demonstrating with a volunteer, I was able to break down this self-consciousness; and they

20

would have waltzed happily through the entire period had I
not called a halt.

I prescribed that the same music be played during the
run-through as that of the band concert taking place in the
park off stage. This sound sparked their rhythms and, in some
cases, their imaginations toward their characters.

Worked individually on:

The Poet

This player, quite short but of striking appearance, and with
large, burning eyes, was shy, and I had expected little from
him. To my delight, he blossomed into his role as the moody
figure who sits at a table composing his verses and in secret
love with Else.

The Tramp

This player is interested in developing a solo form of mime.
Because of this, and as it seemed to me best to begin the play
with a stage free except for the presence of the Waiter, I
contrived a scene in which this character would be the first to
appear. The time was envisioned as that hiatus in the
afternoon shortly before afternoon coffee.

The Tramp enters looking for cigarette butts and discovers
a coin. This emboldens him to seat himself at a table and
order a drink. At display of his wherewithal, he is served,
unenthusiastically, by the Waiter. At the arrival of the
Industrialist he is hastened to finish and depart. A simple
scene contrived for a specific purpose. This player shows a
definite talent, and not only for such roles.

This scene is comparatively easy for a performer, for its
action is unbroken by the necessity of communication with
others, except for the brief encounters with the Waiter. This
is also true in the case of the Poet, which, in essence, is a solo,
without direct communication with the object of his concern.

The Poet scene, while dissimilar in circumstance, recalled
an incident in my own life which also had to do with a poet.
One Sunday when I was a raw beginner, Kalonyme took me to
lunch at a Syrian restaurant on West Street in lower
Manhattan. Except for two Syrian families, only we were

21

present until another person entered; I was only vaguely aware of his presence, as he had seated himself across the room behind our table. Some time later, probably induced by curiosity, I turned my head and saw a youngish man staring straight ahead, seemingly in reflection, with a pencil poised; then he made an entry in a notebook beside him. "There is a poet over there," I said jokingly to K. "It is Cummings," he replied sotto voce.

There is an amusing sidelight to this anecdote, for K. and E. E. Cummings were old friends; but neither, tactfully, acknowledged the other because of my presence, Cummings assuming — and rightly — that K. did not wish intrusion on his privacy at that moment.

A perfect example of the nuances of human exchange of which mime is capable. While I did not think of it in those terms then, no doubt its subtleties made an indelible impression, for even today I remember the avoidance of recognition in the eyes of those two men.

One of the enormous problems of mime, where there must be communication with others, is not to make the audience conscious that verbal communication is missing. With this class I am endeavoring to discover how far this can be accomplished. I am uneasy as to its prospect of success, for I believe that mime has to do only with those nuances of expression for which words are inadequate, and that the moment word is required, it should be employed. I am undertaking this experiment to prove myself wrong, and where it will end remains to be discovered.


## Aside: From Whence?

On tour the TV interviewer asked, "Tell me, how do you get your ideas?" This question is often asked by the press and others, although the phrase more often is: "From where?"

One ought to be prepared with some short, reasonably adequate response, but I am always caught unawares and find myself at a loss. I say "at a loss" because the question seems to presuppose that there is a succinct explanation — a methodical route easily retraceable by others. The truth is that I do not go in search of ideas. I do not know where they hide and must wait for them to find me. When they do come, I accept or reject them or, not immediately grasping their portent, lay them aside to lie in the womb that is memory until some spark causes them to fecundate. Sometimes an idea materializes as if it were a sudden spring shower let loose from an accumulation of thought clouds; at other times it may strike as a sudden gale which, on a fine bright day, blows up from nowhere.

To this interviewer, being again unprepared to meet what experience should have taught was an inevitable question, I committed the unpardonable sin of television and radio: I sat stricken in silence. My inquisitor, happily, was equal to the situation and came to my rescue. "You mean," she said, "that you are just sitting minding your own business and an idea comes and hits you on the head?"

I confessed that it was the perfect answer, and said that I wished I could have thought of it myself.

We laughed in mutual understanding — her perception undoubtedly stemming from her own inability to account for similar sensations — those vagrant thoughts and intuitions which sometimes consolidate into definite form.

Later, remembering this exchange, it seemed to me that the question so often arises because of the popular but mistaken notion that mime involves a process by which the performer goes about with a memory-camera, photographing interesting subjects encountered on travels far and near; or, for lack of a selective eye, translates into mime portraits of characters discovered in history, drama, or literature. Although these are legitimate, if somewhat limiting, sources of material, I do not function in this manner. I do not claim mine is the better route; but mine, though more complex, is the natural one for me. Like a poet, novelist, or dramatist, I become interested in the aspect of a mood or some facet of human behavior, and am led, largely through intuition, to invent a character who will best symbolize what I wish to convey. This character, whatever its visual form, whether abstract or literal, represents not only itself but the age and society in which it lives. The genesis of any character remains a constant in my memory, so that each time I perform it is as though it were revealing itself to me for the first time. I never lose interest in its potentialities, and I take it for granted that the viewer watches with the same obsession with the character that I too have.

The following is an attempt to trace the circuitous route which led to the invention of one character of my theatre: Boy Cardinal.

Following the London theatre season of 1932, several months of travel brought us to rest in Beaulieu on the Côte d'Azur. In those years the Riviera was still more a winter than a summer resort, and we were the only guests at the large, Edwardian Hôtel Beaulieu except for two women who appeared at lunch and dinner: a raven-beaked, provincial countess, encased in black and bedecked with golden chains, and her subdued spinster daughter to whom she rarely spoke.

Affected by the oppressive silence, we would retire after luncheon to take a siesta and to consider whether to transport ourselves to Monte Carlo or Nice for the remainder of the sojourn before sailing for home. On one afternoon during this period of transition, we sat on the terrace, somnolent, and dazed

24

by the relentless, glittering sapphire sea. I thought of how this pair who subdued our spirits was almost identical to another encountered in an equally deserted hotel in Hendaye, where we had stayed briefly before taking off for Spain. The formidable severity of these two mothers and their dour daughters made them appear like apparitions drawn by Balzac; figures changeless through at least several generations, since years to them were only circles endlessly repeated. (These shades secreted themselves into a pocket of my mind until, sometime later, they reappeared to my consciousness and were reborn in quite different form in theatre numbers entitled "End of a World" and "French-Provincial.") They were, in short, spectres from a former era, stranded in the ferment of the post-World War I world.

On this afternoon my thoughts were mainly concerned with Greece, recently visited for the first time. Imbued with all I had seen, I wished to translate my learnings into a retelling of some of the sacred fables — ambitiously planning to play all the characters myself. (It took six years to accomplish this, and its first performances were held at the Metropolitan Museum of Art in New York.) The eyestrain arising from concentrating on these thoughts and at the same time staring out on the blinding sea caused me to turn away for relief.

### Inception of "Boy Cardinal"

The first thing that occurred to me was the dissimilarity in color between the mountains behind Beaulieu and the Castilian plain —

"Ochres, white, terra cotta, black" — Picasso's palette.

25

BLACK? Monet's ghost protests! But black is a combination of the three primaries — mix them and what do you get? A good, rich
black.

Toledo — first view — still rising out of the plain as El Greco saw it — the weather cooperated — providing
storm clouds hovering over the crown.
On the other hand
It stood on the plain — a cone Virgin —
diademed with the Alcazar —
like
those figures of Her, stiff-robed — set on platforms
carried through the streets in Holy Week.
Madre Dolorosa — weeping.
The spire of the Cathedral pierced a cloud, and it rained as we drove up and through the Moorish gate to the top.
The whitewashed rectangle — Chapel — the diffused white light —
wonderful for painting
First it served the Moors
Then the Jews
Then the Church
Now
a museum for tourists with El Greco's saints agonizing on the walls. El Greco, of whom the handsome old guide — bearded — in Granada spoke condescendingly as a foreigner and therefore unequal to any Spanish painter, particularly Ribera and Zurbarán. Not a glimmer of gratitude —
After all — the honor was all the Greek's for having been
Accepted.
The interior of the Cathedral —

26

Too dark to decipher its architectural wonders
              And empty
Except
      a young priest, walking diagonally across
              turned (without stopping)
                  looked
      Who were we?
                  Foreigners —
REMINISCENT — of what?
          Oh yes!
O. and I, after a long walk, had dropped in to rest in
St. Patrick's.
                  When?
Must have been sometime shortly before my first
performance.
                  We were the only ones except for the
                  inevitable old woman praying.
                  And
another young priest walked — also in diagonal line —
toward a door on the far side of the nave.
          And —
without stopping, turned to look at us with
casual curiosity.
                  I winked at him
              It took a moment to soak in
                  then
                      his pace slowed, he turned —
          Unbelieving — eyes wide met mine —
                  turned quickly and hastened his pace and
                                      disappeared.
"You are naughty!" O. reproved — but entertained.

27

"He didn't mind," I told her flippantly, for in his glance I
had seen the eyes of a man, not a priest.

                      For an instant he almost smiled.

"The Pavana" needs an accent to its period
              Something about the Church.
                    St. Teresa?

Too obvious — besides, a nun unless sentimentally
portrayed is a touchy subject. Hands off!
              That walk of the priests —
conditioned in rhythm by incessant chant of the Mass of
prayers.

WERE I A MAN
             I would dosomethingabout a priest.

                THIS INFERNAL SUNLIGHT

The aqueous light through the rounds of bottle-bottom
glass in the windows of the Borgia apartments in the Vatican
which kept out the blistering sun
                    and spying eyes.

        Small secret rooms — conducive to intrigue.
Cesare Borgia was only eighteen when made a cardinal of
Spain by his father, the Pope.
                 Didn't I read — somewhere —
that in the sixteenth century (time of "Pavana") a young noble-
man — nineteen —
was made Cardinal of Toledo? Scarcely more than a boy.
      I CANNOT BE A MAN BUT I COULD BE A BOY.
             A BOY CARDINAL
               Why not?

                            There he is —
arrogant — his flanks moving freely under his robe.
        THAT WALK!

"Boy Cardinal"

It is part of his ritual — ingrained — just as the walk of a matador is part of *his*.

  Both have the measured tread of a *paso doble* — that one played at the corrida in Málaga — the best one.

  If I can't find it I'll have to write down what I remember — will require something else composed to take the place of the too sweet section that all *paso dobles* seem to have.

    That walk

      feet in matador's slippers —

pressure of the stone which is his earth on the soles — sending up sap into his body.

    HERE HE COMES

a narrow ruff around his neck to frame his face

      and

to set him back in time — sixteenth-century Spain.

Cardinals and matadors wear capes

  the Devil and the bull have horns

    from which

  Cardinal and matador must escape

    but

He is a boy and not yet conditioned to a life of deprivation

    besides —

There is plenty of precedent in history.

      Here he comes — with a fine lace handkerchief

      stuffed in his sleeve. Symbol of worldliness?

In the cathedral in Seville one afternoon, a choir boy coming from rehearsal with his fellow singers blew his nose in his surplice and all, like pigeons, were shooed out by their choirmaster. They were enchanting. In Holy Week they perform a dance on the altar, a ritual of hundreds of years — and accompany themselves with castanets. Cardinal Richelieu

danced to such self-accompaniment too — but not in church!
At balls.

> The Boy Cardinal might use them too — to express
> thoughts he
> dare not utter.

> > Here he comes —
> > HERE HE IS

## Aside: Mirror, Mirror on the Wall

It is the custom for dancers to practice before a mirror so that
they may have a view of their *line* — this both to check technical rightnesses and to reveal the image which they are presenting to the audience.

A dancer of dramatic roles has recently stated in an inter-
view that prior to a performance she sits before the mirror and
watches the transformation of her face into that of the character.

In mime, such preparation for a role would be disastrous,
except perhaps in the case of a highly stylized form; for otherwise it would serve only to flatten the character and deprive it
of dimension.

Character is not something which comes into being backstage in front of a mirror. In mime, the ultimate success in the
presentation of a thought or emotion lies in the punctuation
of the elements which lead to its resolution. It lies, as in a
poem or a sentence, in the *cumulative* presentation of the
thought, which does not develop — which has almost no meaning — without its transitional line. It is the transitional line on
which the viewer concentrates and which heightens his ex-

pectation or surprise at its outcome. It is this which keeps him in suspense.

I myself am deflected by working before a mirror, for I am distracted at seeing my person, which is dissimilar to the creature of my imagination. Technically speaking, watching what one does means that the eyes are focussed into one's own, and this denies freedom to the vision of the character. When I perform, I am no more than a necessary physical instrument. As I respond to the character, I see it in clear perspective, and am fascinated by its revelation of itself, like that of a person unobserved. At the same time, since it can come to life only through my physical self, I am the pencil or brush through which it transmits its meaning to me as the viewer. To me this is a tactile communication.

## Log: Fifth Session

The time has come when I must discover of what their former technical trainings consist, for I do not see much evidence that they have had sufficient preparation to be able to receive what little I may have to offer. One thing apparent is that their previous training has not afforded them either physical or inventive release. Toward this end, suggested that, instead of beginning cold with the play, we start with a few warm-up exercises.

Enthusiastic approval at the prospect of being given something tangible to grasp. As I suspected, the endeavor to translate into concrete expression the elusive thoughts of capricious imagination has proved both wearing and mystifying.

Since the last session, and for the first time, I have examined the basis of my own physical preparation and have found that I have, indeed, from my own requirements, evolved a technique through habit. Whether this conditioning, useful to me, will prove of value to them remains to be seen.

As the human body can move only within its own orbit, all exercises are fundamentally the same in that they have to do with liberation of movement. However, there is a vast difference in the point of view toward which the liberation must function. Mime, generally speaking, requires more detailed control than does dance, which is more flamboyant in its physical expression. The mime-as-actor conceals rather than reveals his technical proficiencies. It is a subtle difference of intent, and this is not to say that one form of theatre is superior to another but only that each dictates its own requirements.

It is natural to me to begin each period of work with rediscovery of my skeletal structure as an impersonal instrument. This habit, I believe, came about from an attempt to free myself from tenseness after hours at the easel or at the writing desk. From a standing position, well-balanced, I re-examine *very slowly* the way each bone moves in its socket — up and down or rotating, as in a well-oiled ball bearing. I begin with the head, then the spine, then the limbs to their extremities. *I listen* with my senses to the workings of this machine. I do this both standing and lying flat on the floor. I find it is wonderfully relaxing and rids me of the nervous mannerisms personal to me.

Now, and again slowly, I stretch, bend, and swing, with a view to sensing the tensile possibilities of the muscles, cognizant of the fact that they must be treated as gently as elastic bands.

Then, to any music which happens to be playing on the radio, I improvise exercises in counterpoint to what I hear, exercises which include accelerating or diminishing speeds or exaggerated movements.

Since it is not my aim to fall into a set habit of movement, these inventions are rarely duplicated. In this way I have accustomed myself to endless variations of tempi and movements. The inventions are not transposed literally and

34

made part of the composition of a theatre character; instead they are used to ingrain flexibility and responsiveness in my body, so that each character will have complete freedom to discover its own rhythm.

As these exercises are performed, I become instinctively aware of the phrasing of each gesture and movement and am given a sense of dramatic composition, since anything I hear in music is taken as a unit within which to work. I am, in fact, an auxiliary instrument playing in counterpoint to what I hear in a private jam session.

Through these means, I am rid of myself as an individual by the time I am ready to work on an idea.

Of course, such procedure is inadequate for anyone who wishes to form a uniform, recognizable style, as it is not conducive to establishing repetitive habit of movement, such as is necessary in stylized forms of dance or mime. It is only a way which I have discovered, for my own purpose, as the best to rid the characters I perform of identity with myself as an individual.

Began the group with skeletal exercises and watched their faces fill with amazement at discovering the stiffness of their joints. Their laughter was pained when I told them that they were all potential arthritics! Even the dancers were astonished to find their arms aching after rotating the fingers. But in mime, sense of touch is of utmost importance. The touch of an idea — the feel of space.

At the end of this exercise they all yawned deeply — a good sign, for it showed that they were no longer tense.

After this I indulged them with exercises more familiar to them — moving, bending, stretching, etc. — which they enjoyed. But during the rest period before the brief run-through (which was all we had time for), I saw most of them contemplating and moving their fingers with a new delight.

Thus endeth the Fifth Session.

## Log: Sixth Session

Began with a run-through and found little progress since last
session except more ease in following the pattern of blocking
— the result of repetition.

The Poet and the Tramp are the only ones not at sea
without the aid of words and I suspect also that they are
the only ones who have experimented on their own at home.
Their interpretations are more imaginative and subtle, and they
seem to grasp the clues toward mime which I throw out at
random more quickly than the others.

The "Woman of the World," a player of some stock
experience, ventured the idea that it would be "easier to get
into the mood" in costume. All agreed.

This expressed longing for costume emphasized what I
have come to suspect; that they believe mime a charade in
which dress is a mask under which they would feel free to
disport themselves, as in a *bal masque;* a disguise without
which they feel naked.

I am beginning to see in another light the reasons why in
the first session they found pleasure in their assumption that
not being burdened with a strict technical formula would
lighten their studies. Little do they suspect what lies ahead for
them, for to invent is far more difficult than to follow a rule by
rote.

What they require is a scouring of the rust off their
imaginative power, to make it gleam!

Told them: That you feel naked without costume means
only that you are self-conscious. Please remember that to be
self-conscious is a waste of time, for the audience has no
interest in your personal problems. It is too busy concentrating
on trying to grasp what you are telling them about the
character you portray. It will resent any deflection from this
by the intrusion of self-consciousness on your part. Moreover,
the audience is only a sounding board which sends back to
you, as the performer, the tonal qualities your character
projects to it.

## The Audience

The audience is sensitive to sham. While it may not analyze
its uneasiness, it senses your uncertainties. It is cruel and
unforgiving, and once the thread of its intentness is broken,
it is difficult to knot it together again. Remember yourselves
as members of an audience and whether this has not been true
in your own experience.

I am reminded of an incident witnessed recently in Paris.
A remarkable and noted mime did not receive an expected
laugh; instead of continuing, he broke the line of his character
by turning his head slightly more toward the audience,
repeated the smile, exaggerated, which turned it into a
strained grimace. The audience laughed — but *at* the
performer, not *with* the character. The thread was broken, and
what followed was lost for a full minute before this personal
injection was forgotten. An example of the disastrous effect of a
performer's self-conscious worry that his character has missed
its aim.

Actually he was mistaken, for the initial grin of surprise by
the character had not passed unnoticed but had been received
with appreciative smiles and a few chuckles. However, it had
not been sufficiently prepared for dramatically to warrant an
outburst of laughter and thus was taken only as an incident
on the road to more decisive comic resolution. They were right.

Never underestimate an audience, for its unpredictable
responses may be more perceptive than you think!

After this detour, since I was eager to get on with the play, I
conceded them their wish for costumes, although costumes had
not seemed to me to be necessary at this point. It was, it
develops, the women rather than the men who were concerned
with this aspect of performing. Made suggestions as to how
summer frocks could be given undestructive alterations —
lengthening of hems, belts etc. — to indicate the period of the
play until we were more prepared for performance, when
expenditure for acquiring and making costumes could be
considered.

The question then arose as to whether I rehearse in costume, and this threw me into an account of my personal approach.

## Costumes

I dislike the word "costume," for to me it connotes apparel designed by a specialist in that field to conform to an over-all picture of a production. While I realize the legitimacy of a cohesive pictorial effect, too often in viewing a play performers do not seem at home in the dress of their characters: this is also true of some women, who in private life seem lay-figures of their dressmakers.

The history of dress throughout the ages is open to anyone through volumes on the subject in public libraries or through the simple expedient of looking at photographs of apparel, paintings, or sculptures, dating back to the very inception of the craft of dressmaking. But to wear historical garb requires understanding, not only of the dress itself, but of the person who wears it and of the society in which he lives.

My own case in the theatre is quite different from those performers who must wear dress supplied by others, for I make the clothes worn by my characters. In a way I cannot claim to have designed them, for these characters, from their inception, appear to me dressed according to their own taste — they point out to me, rather than I to them, how they prefer to be seen. Often I try to exert my prerogative as their creator and strive to change their image, for I have the added preoccupation of having to visualize their inevitable place on the program, and I may conceive of something more strikingly complementary in line and color; and sometimes a character will concede a touch of color that the program calls for, but by and large, these figures refuse to come to life in anything contrary to their own tastes.

I have been sent gifts of wonderful gowns, perfect in period for one of my numbers, but I have never been able to use them because the character has found them inacceptable. The characters of other players may not be as finicky as mine, but this is the way it is for me.

Since I know from the start what they will wear, and the quality of fabrics involved, it is not necessary for me to work in costume while evolving their actions, for I know the costumes — their line, weight, and the way their folds will fall in natural movement. I do have one rule about any draperies, and that is never to manipulate them for pictorial effect beyond the natural demands of the character. I find it distracting as a member of the audience when it is obvious that a player is conscious of disturbing the line of a drapery or when these are arranged for calculated line. I prefer to let them fall where they will according to the movement and mood of the character, without any interference by me. The end result is better, both sculpturally and dramatically.

Am finding that once I get started talking I am inclined to go on following a line of thought, and today went on in this vein. Told them: Release yourselves to the dictates of the character as you see it, and do not be afraid to make a mistake — do not think that you are making fools of yourselves — for you will learn more through error than success. Every time you feel yourself temporarily successful, you will find yourself at a dead end; for every idea has to be reborn in its fulfillment. Mistakes are a springboard from which to dive into discovery of their cause. I may be able to point out falsities in your character — but only according to my own sensibility, which may be incompatible with yours. If you feel uneasy in a character, you must discover for yourself the *why*. The road

39

to invention is arduous except at those times when an image may appear full-panoplied — like Athene. But if you are not willing to take on and develop this image, you do not belong in the theatre; for no director can, in the end, supply you with imagination.

### Imagination

What is imagination?

It is a thought which appears unexpectedly from the treasure hoard of memory, like a shooting star in the night heavens which, before disappearing into black space, leaves in the mind's eye the phosphorescent streak of an idea in its wake: conjectures as to its source and destination.

Everything experienced in life — whether seen, dreamt, smelled, felt, or read — is stored in memory; and all is recalled in some form at subsequent times. Imagination makes all time present. Through imagination we understand the past and present and invent views of the future.

Our inventions are the embroidering of our memories. Without imagination, nothing experienced has meaning.

To understand the modes and manners of any age, including those of our own society, requires that through imagination we come to understand the reasons behind the behavior; for a mime cannot function if he views habits outside his own as oddities — like the tourist who finds foreign customs different from what he is used to and therefore unreasonable.

After this peroration, thought it advisable to land them on earth, noting that they were stimulated rather than, as I had feared, depressed.

Mentioned that one of the symptoms of their uneasiness was that in walking they retained their own characteristics, and that therefore it might be helpful to examine the principles of walking. Asked them first to rest by walking freely and naturally about the studio — a release which they welcomed. With Machiavellian, ends-justify-the-means cunning, at a point when they seemed, like children at play, completely oblivious of my presence, I said as casually as possible, "See whether you can sense your own individual manner of walking — concentrate on it." After a time of this self-examination, the result of which was for each one to exaggerate his habit as he became more and more aware of it, they began to notice the habits of one another and to point them out.

Stopped this game to examine the principle of walking — divested of mannerisms or, in other words, character.

Had them perform, with even transference of balance, walking to a set beat. They were surprised to find it difficult to retain balance.

Pointed out that this exercise was not without practical purpose, for there were times in the theatre when an even progression with a direct line was essential: for example, where a formal, majestic line was required, or where the intrusion of personal mannerisms could cause an unintentional comic effect, as in the case of women in long formal dress.

These two examples illustrated another important point: that the mimist must take into account not only the natural behavior of the character but also the over-all mood of the scene. This brought up the question of "realism," a hangover from their dramatic-school training.

Told them: If you have occasion to see a play from the audience, a play in which the characters walk and behave with what appears unfettered realism, and then to see it again from the wings, you will discover that what seemed to you as viewer so "natural" from the front is achieved by contrived design. This is part of the art of acting and mime. In all professional performing, where constant repetition of performance is required, nothing can be left to chance except the ability to make adjustments to unforeseen circumstances.

41

The most realistic play or mime is as set in its form as any stylized school of dance, although it is part of the art of the mime-as-actor to give the audience a sense that the performance is being improvised before its eyes. The ACCIDENT OF THE MOMENT.

To make any gesture or step appear accidental requires complete physical control over the behavior of the character. He moves and behaves according to his own logic, not yours. For this reason you must divorce yourselves from your habit of walking, but ONLY ONSTAGE. Once you have achieved a sense of balance in the mechanics of walking, you will have a basis on which to improvise the mannerisms of your character. The mime divorces intuitively from the figure he portrays, and must be physically ready for and mentally attuned to the erratic behavior of the character he performs, erraticisms logical to the character.

It is becoming a habit to talk too much in an endeavor to unsettle their complacency. As parting shot, said what I believe to be true:

Much is said about "the art of acting." Of what does this consist? The playwright supplies the play, which the director translates into action, explaining his interpretation to the actors and designing their movements. The actor reads his lines as explained to him with all the understanding and vocal technique at his command; but in the end, his creative contribution to the play is as mime. This is the visual image he presents to the audience; in this is embodied all his understanding of the character. It is the behavior of the character by which the audience understands the play visually. The way the character walks, stands, sits, listens — all reveal the meaning of his words. All the nuances of his speech have little meaning unless accompanied by an effective visual portrait. It is here that he becomes a creative collaborator, for here he reveals the character as an individual human being. No small responsibility, for it requires the ability to make the character come to life for the audience, by actions as well as words. Acting is a combination of intelligent reading of lines and MIME! Mime, used with discretion, only to enhance the playwright's words. It is an exacting art.

## Aside: Mime Versus Mimicry

The Mime creates a character. The mimic is an imitator.
The one creates; the other copies.
Chaplin is a mime; those who imitate him are mimics.

### Variations on the Theme

During my early years in the theatre, a noted actress came backstage after a performance: a dramatic figure, enveloped in a long black cape and with the bearing of a Star. I was impressed by her presence and, of course, flattered by her comments. After speaking about the performance, she made an eloquent gesture embracing the other waiting visitors and said, "I should think that you would do a take-off of all this — you know — the artist and her public backstage."

I was taken aback at so ordinary an idea — or so it seemed to me — from one noted for her roles in classical tragedy. Moreover, I was mystified as to what she had seen in my performance that led her to believe that the idea would interest me. I could not be so rude as to say that I did not go about making mental photographs of persons for future mimicry, as I invented my own characters and ideas. Not wishing to seem ungrateful, I engaged in one of those deceits of social intercourse by pretending the idea was interesting.

43

Her keen ear must have caught a strained note of insincerity in my pale attempt at enthusiasm, for, after a searching glance, her face congealed into an impersonal mask, and a gauze of mutual antagonism separated us.

A year or two later, lying in a tub in a Vienna hotel reading Proust's account of the acknowledgment by the Duchesse de Guermantes of the introduction to her of a noted historian and himself, I laughed aloud, for it recalled the nuances of the exchange between the actress and me. It was not that I identified Proust's characters with either of us, but that I associated the chilly climates that had arisen in both instances.

The idea offered by the actress lay stillborn, but memory of the exchange, recalled by Proust's powerful descriptive language, opened a vista of other possibilities on the subject of snobbism.

## Variation Two

One night in the early thirties, on first curtain call at the end of the opening number, I was distracted by what appeared to be a row of miniature spotlights shining up from the front row. I concluded that it was an optical illusion, an aftereffect from the glare of balcony spots, abetted by opening night nerves. On second call I saw that it was a solid row of opera glasses, in which the stage lights were reflected. It seemed odd that an entire front row, at least half of whom were men, should find glasses necessary, but I decided that these investigators of my face were playgoers whose interest lay more in the personality of the player than in what was being done.

Later, I mentioned the incident to K., who said, "You've never met them, but that was the x–x crowd studying acting!" That so serious and respected a group thought to discover a method in my mime by such inspection was startling, for the truth was that concentration on that limited area must have obscured rather than revealed what I was doing.

Mime is not a technical stunt.

## Aside: Anent "Realistic Symbolism"

While the following anecdote has nothing to do with mime directly, it does indicate one of the hazards encountered in an attempt to establish a mood — in this case, mood through sound.

Judith Anderson and I went to see a play given professional production by a group of young Actor's Studio players. Shortly before the house lights dimmed, a faint, rapid, tapping sound issued from behind the curtain. The audience, perplexed, quieted for a moment; then, probably believing as I did that the sound had to do with last-minute repairs, resumed their chatter. The tapping continued as the house lights dimmed, and I concluded it was a typewriter. Judith whispered to me, "What's that?" I said, "It's a typewriter — they're establishing the mood." She replied wryly, "They're rewriting the play." Her wit was sharper than that of the director who had devised this badly calculated effect.

*In mime, one must stimulate the imagination of the audience — not befuddle it.*

# Log: Seventh Session

Have come to view the play solely as a basis from which to give detailed exposition of technical problems involved in the portrayal of character. Came to this conclusion since, between sessions, new facets of their weaknesses occur to me, and much time is spent conceiving and experimenting with ways that these can be overcome. I will not have them perform after a term with me in a manner which I cannot condone. I could get them more directly into shape for public viewing by having them imitate my demonstrations of each character, but this would be of little value to them in the future. Besides, I have no intention of doing their work for them, a danger too apparent.

The slim suggestion that tourists send postcards home brought the player assigned to the role of the Tourist equipped with postcards and a handbag. So that she might familiarize herself with these objects, asked her to come into the café, seat herself at the table, and address the cards — as herself, with no character in mind. She, the most timid of all the players, gained confidence by having a definite duty to perform. She accomplished the task simply and directly, without self-consciousness — although the cards were to her, or so appeared to us who watched, merely bits of cardboard on which she scribbled a few hasty words, laid down her pencil, and waited.

Asked the group for comments. Someone noted that the cards had not been addressed, and another offered the information that they had not been stamped. Primitive observations!

I had deliberately kept from suggesting any image of the character, in the hope that an idea would be offered on which to improvise. Nothing came forth.

Said: That is true, but those are details. The first thing to consider is that the addressing of postcards is not interesting to watch unless the writer appears to be setting down a personal message. Everything performed in mime must have

46

personal meaning to the character, consciously or unconsciously. This meaning must be projected to the viewer, visually. That is, your thoughts or those of your character must be projected by your manner of behavior.

The player asked whether "PLEASE" would I not show how this could be done, and the others shouted "YES."

Although it was entirely against the principle that all invention was to be left to them, I softened in the hope that what I did would launch them into inventive flight. Merely to address these cards myself seemed pointless in relation to the play, which I wanted to get under way. Thus I invented possibilities according to the first image that came to mind, which was that of a youngish woman on a lonely holiday.

On the way to the wings, I had the advantage over the players of kaleidoscopic recall of a summer spent at a resort on the cold, pale blue, Baltic coast. The time was the last gasp of the twenties; and despite unsettling evidence of the growing new Germany, to me the pervading aroma was that of Thomas Mann's childhood summer in Travemünde as recounted in *Buddenbrooks.*

## Improvisation on Theme of Tourist

(*Attempted division of thoughts of A. E. as performer and Tourist as character*)

A.E. (On way to wings): "How *triste*" was that resort. German *traurigkeit!* Undercurrent of their nature — cruel, too. This Hotel — provincial first class — but the Tourist has the least expensive room. Unmarried — timid — lonely — escaped from a grey-stone small town in a bold decision. About twenty-four — bad age for an unmarried woman in a small town. Shift entrance further upstage

47

to make her appear as if strolling from a distance — the park where the band is playing. Prettyish but not strikingly — will become quite plain — later — depending on what happens to her — hair neat, no sense of coquettry — an escaped ringlet? Tan skirt — four inches above ankles — modest length — but a fresh white dotted Swiss blouse with a blue taffeta ribbon bow at throat? Black belt — tight — to accentuate rhythm of walk — affected by music — large soft black handbag — serviceable! (*In place*) Here I go — come from the park — purse swinging along with music.

*Tourist:* What a wonderful band — if I were alone I'd waltz and waltz . . . oh! here I am already at the terrace.

A.E.: Too little space for change of mood — retime.

*Tourist:* Those two girls on the promenade — friends — talking and giggling — if they see me, I'll smile — they might smile back — even invite me to join them. They didn't see me. . .

A.E.: Flirt comes — alone — young lovers behind.

*Tourist:* There is that FLIRT — she only looks at men — and that boy and girl — they never notice anyone.

A.E.: Short, resigned sigh for transference. Examine terrace.

*Tourist:* There they all are — talking-talking-talking — having coffee and *torte* — looks good. . .

(A.E.: *Spies empty table*)

There is an empty table — but to pass all those people — well, why not? — I stay at this hotel too — pay. . .

(A.E.: *Transfers bag from hand to arm — deep breath of determination — holds it to propel to table — chair position bad — swings it to face* DOWN — *sight line of house — sits — exhales — heart is palpitating — quick breath to relax — looks about — brightly*)

48

*Tourist:* That elegant couple — probably from Berlin — she is looking at me — I'll smile and nod — that was a mistake — she nodded — but not friendly — thought me bold — do not do it again. . .

(A.E.: *Remember this exchange — Woman's glance vaguely amused — turns to speak to companion — he glances at girl — impersonally — and away — girl looks swiftly about to conceal embarrassment*)

*Tourist:* The tables are separate islands — people only interested in themselves — how much they all have to talk about! Here comes the waiter — I'll just have coffee.

(A.E.: *Waiter has come for order — already has large coffee pot, cup, sugar, etc. on tray — also plate of cakes. Looks at her inquiringly. She nods — but refuses cake. Does not raise head — looks up at him only with eyes — smiles — apologetically shakes head. He is resigned to her as a negligible client but is not unkind — puts three lumps of sugar in her saucer*)

*Tourist:* He does not like it that I do not have coffee and *torte* every day — like the others — I feel conspicuous having it alone. . .

(A.E.: *Puts in two lumps — stirs — tastes — adds the third*)

*Tourist:* That's better — it's good — good and hot. . . How much money do I have left?

(A.E.: *Reasonable tourist preoccupation — counts what is in her wallet — does not take it out — puts wallet back, reassured — takes out postcards — picture side to the audience — looks at them — approvingly*)

*Tourist:* They are pretty. . .

(A.E.: *What now? Establish some connection with someone. Who? Looks about — catches eye of Prostitute*

looking at her — from DOWN LEFT — smiles — Prostitute
smiles in return )

*Tourist:* What a nice girl — friendly. . . Think that I'll address
the cards — they'll see that I have friends too.

(A.E.: *Searches and finds pencil in handbag. Ten cards
too many — six at most*)

*Tourist:* Who will I send them to? Uncle — the aunts — Frau
Schmidt — Elsa — maybe I'll think of someone else.

(A.E.: *Sorts cards — no more than six — puts one aside
— the best — three the same. . . How would it be if she
held the cards, pictures facing her as if they were a hand
at cards? — she is slightly more animated now. Remembering the Prostitute, she glances playfully at her and
smiles again, cards in hand — Prostitute smiles — a little
less this time — says something to her companion — the
Gigolo — his back to Tourist. He turns, looks quickly
and away*)

*Tourist:* She smiled again. Uncle and aunts first. . .

(A.E.: *Writes short message on each, and addresses —
quickly — businesslike — does not stamp — takes too
much time although audience would laugh — but less
the second, less the third time*)

*Tourist:* Frau Schmidt next — this view of the sea. . .

(A.E.: *Be sure audience can see each picture side.
Thinks for a moment — short message — more prim —
address*)

*Tourist:* Now Elsa.

(A.E.: *View of the hotel. Writes more gayly — as though
holiday an enormous success — turns card over, searches
and finds her window — marks with an* x — *not clear
enough — moistens pencil with lips and retraces lines.
Now quite animated. Places finished card on pile with*

50

*others — evens pile — to neaten. Picks up last card —
pictures of bandstand at sunset. To whom? Then, in
sudden daring...)*
*Tourist:* To Oswald. He danced with me twice at the party —
and brought me a glass of punch — if only I'd waited
longer maybe he would have walked me home...

    (A.E.: *This message difficult to formulate, with breaks
to think — face nervous — tender. At end signs "Love"
— quickly — starts to address — stops — takes tiny address book from handbag on her lap — bag is in her
way — in gesture of unnatural carelessness puts bag —
open — on chair back of table — finds address — puts it
on card — takes sip of coffee after this fit of daring. Re-
flects — rereads card — erases indiscreet ending — pencil must have eraser — rewrites another word — deep
breath intake — kisses card softly — places on pile. Exhales — upstage elbow on table, head on hand — with
downstage hand keeps time dreamily — eyes closed —
to music of band)*

END

    The above account of the improvisation is a much simpli-
fied version of what actually takes place, for in mime the character is revealed simultaneously both as the performer sees it
and as the character sees itself. It is a contrapuntal duet in
which the performer, fascinated by the character, discovers its
many facets, while the character is unaware of the existence of
the performer and of the fact that it is being observed by anyone. Were this duet to be truly set down in words, the form
would be indecipherable, as the words indicating the thoughts
of each would have to be superimposed. I am certain that any
performer who *knows* what he is doing understands this truth;

and I venture to set forth the relationship between the performer and his character in so literal a fashion only because of the recurrent question asked by viewers, professional or lay: "What do you think about while you perform?"

In me, the nuances of the meanings and behavior of every character of my particular form of mime arouse constant wonder — they are a source of rediscovery with each performance, even though the outward form remains unchanged, or so it appears.

It is this which, I believe, keeps alive characters performed hundreds of times — characters which, I must assume, continue to interest viewers to whom they are familiar and who express disappointment if they fail to appear on a program.

I myself, as a member of the audience of any art form, prefer not to be distracted by obvious technical contrivances. I want first to see *what* is done, not *how;* for when the *how* demands primary notice, the personality of the perpetrator injects itself to the detriment of his intention. That is, I prefer that technique which can be discovered and marvelled at only later, in afterthought.

Discussion of the improvisation filled remaining time. Asked for other possibilities, as my rough draft had only been a starting point from which to attack the problem, which was that of retaining the interest of the audience while addressing postcards. The group, however, now saw the Tourist only in the terms just outlined. I pointed out a particular fault in the improvisation — that, as performed by me, she might be too similar in nature to Else. To achieve a more effective contrast, she might be a figure in mourning, isolated from the others by her sorrow; and in that case the addressing of the cards would be shorter and more melancholy. She would pass through the scene more briefly and, after having coffee whilst addressing the cards, would disappear into the hotel, oblivious of the others although she was observed by them with curiosity. Lost in her thoughts, she would move through the scene unaware of the world about her, like a somnambulist.

While the idea appealed to me, it did not so affect the group, who did not visualize this more dramatic note in the structure of the play. The player to whom the role of the Tourist had been assigned was reluctant to make the transference to a different character from the one just seen; and I was unwilling to continue improvising, as this could only delay their own coming to grips with the physical problems involved in mime. Learning by watching is like listening to a description of the effect of heat. Experience is necessary for true appreciation.

Against further delaying of their practical experience, I acceded to their wish. This meant taking my spontaneous improvisation and fitting it in organically with the rest of the play. The Tourist had been left onstage stranded and lost in thought. Now the denouement . . .

What stood out in memory were several unresolved facts: that she, normally precise, had left her purse open on a chair; and that, from the care with which she had counted the contents of her wallet, it could be presumed that her funds were limited. (In mime, nothing is done outside the meaning of the character. In mime, there is no place for excursions into technical display such as dance legitimately affords.)

In the case of the Tourist, the longing to make friends made her gullible to the advances of any adventurer. She had been taken in by the indifferent, good-natured smile of the Prostitute, who recognized her as an *Innocent*. The Prostitute might have noted the open purse on the chair and murmured its existence to the Gigolo, who was not above being a sneak thief. Remembered that, in my mind's eye, he had taken a quick glance at the situation. Let us now assume that, seeing her lost in thought, he takes the wallet with swift fingers, and disappears down the promenade. To make this possible, the other guests should have finished and gone into the hotel — to dress for dinner — while the townspeople should have gone in their own direction. It is now sunset, and the band ends its performance with a last flourish, a flourish which brings the Tourist back to reality — and to the discovery first that her handbag is open on the chair, then that her wallet is gone.

She is now distraught; she searches about under the table and retraces her steps from her entrance — with no help from the waiter, who shrugs off all responsibility and leaves her alone.

Let us consider that the Gigolo may also be a procurer, and that with the aid of the Prostitute he befriends her, taking her off — she trustingly — for their own nefarious purpose. She had now grown in my imagination to embody one theme of early twentieth-century literature and drama, wherein an inexperienced woman is led through innocence to a dreadful end.

This design was accepted with enthusiasm, even by those who had as yet no specific part in its evolution.

The melodramatic conclusion, so alien to the "wiseness" of contemporary girls, will, I hope, inspire an exercise in period study. "Once they can become mesmerized by a pervading mood," I thought, "they may find a root for the evolution of any character."

Remainder of the session spent on the mechanics of how the wallet could be taken without attracting attention.

## Log: Eighth Session

Was greeted with requests from other players for similar help
with their roles. Refused, for the reason (stated once again)
that the play was an exercise in invention for them — not for
me. This plunged them into that state of dilemma which an
explorer might feel when, spying through the trees what
appears to be a clearing of the forest, he discovers it is no more
than a small opening in a jungle.

They will have to be led by the hand, like children.

## Aside: Extensions Infinite

All along the Merritt Parkway, skeleton trees stood engraved
against the ghostly whites·and greys of the winter afternoon,
recalling medical charts of the human nervous system. But,
despite family characteristics, each tree was an individual unto
itself, its growth conditioned to circumstance. In some, roots
had had to feel their way to sources of nourishment around
boulders, which resulted in distorted figures. Sometimes a
tree, rooted in overly close proximity to another, leaned its
body away from the stronger one. The elements also had had
an effect, for only those trunks that were deeply rooted grew
straight — although they too, in their smaller branches, showed
the effect of storms. Even carefully nurtured and groomed
lawn evergreens, some of which at casual glance appeared
identical twins, had, one noted, individual personalities.

Dined that evening at the home of Dr. I. M. Tarlov, the
noted neurosurgeon. One of the guests was a beautiful young
Chinese woman who, Dr. Tarlov informed, was engaged in
the exacting work of making detailed drawing of nerves. Told

him of the deep impression of the barren trees and the thoughts they had aroused, and was rewarded with a wonderfully graphic and startling description of the extensions of the human nervous system. There were, he said, untold myriads of nerve ganglia beyond microscopic detection: more than stars in the universe and more than grains of sand on a beach.

Later, at home, contemplating Dr. Tarlov's remarks, it occurred to me that powerful personal experiences likewise have countless extensions — they stretch out like fingers into the future, triggering new ideas and reactions; often, in the heat of discovering a new idea, we tingle with the excitement of the present, but somewhere back in the spine of our memory is stored the experience of which this "new" idea is only a branch.

This train of thought led into reflections of sensations persistent from childhood which, at that moment, seemed to have some bearing on my approach to mime. To this end I recount only a few experiences which, I believe, had permanent effect, since they persist in memory.

In childhood, sight of the first thrust of a young green shoot from the earth was — a miracle of beauty. The way the moist earth gave way by degrees to the force of the sprouting seed was to me a compelling message of the intention of that plant to GROW; and this sense of wonder toward nature remained constant with me, and has manifested itself in many ways. To this day, an image appearing as unexpectedly as that first sprout on a spring morning arouses in me that exciting sense of the will to grow.

I do not believe that initiation into recognition of the life force was individual to me at that early age, but only that its memory may have persisted because on me, as an only child and without companions my own age, solitary discoveries made an indelible impression.

The inanimate toys of the playroom did not interest me so much as sharing in the adult pleasures of my indulgent parents, who sometimes took me with them to their parties in city or country, or to the theatre, or on shopping excursions for clothes or fabrics, some of which went toward my wardrobe. My parents were both young and had no theories about my upbringing except that I should be healthy and well-mannered. I did, however, before being enrolled in kindergarten, learn to make out the letters of the alphabet and a few words — by watching my mother trace these while reading me the adventures of "Baby Goose." I also remember, distinctly, sitting on my father's chest as he lay on the sofa on Christmas Eve during my year in kindergarten, and following his finger in a child's book of German verse, and singing with him Goethe's refrain "Röslein, Röslein, Röslein rot" while waiting for my mother to end her conference with Santa Claus behind the double door which separated us.

At the age of seven to eight I was already familiar with the feel of fabrics from pieces given to me to sew for my dolls. At that age also, I felt for the first time an intuitive sense of the timelessness of time. This began with a visit with my father to a museum, where I was shown an Egyptian mummy and was told that it was three thousand years old — an extent of time which I could not comprehend and which terrified me by its enormity. During the same visit, my father pointed out to me particular stars far away in the night heavens, and this had the disastrous effect of adding to my terror of time and space beyond the nest of my home. My bewildered parents, fearing that I was in a precarious state of health and mind, resorted to tonics believed to steady the nerves.

In the period of transition from childhood to adolescence another landmark in my consciousness appeared. At school we were informed that the ion within the atom sparks the electric basis for all life. While I didn't really understand how this could be so, nevertheless, it was a revelation which affected me, especially when I considered that even things like rocks embodied this miracle. However naïve may have been this impression, my new knowledge did give me a sense of contact with the world. To my primitive understanding, everything touched, heard, seen, or smelled was an exciting symbol of a living world.

The recounting of these incidents would have no purpose were it not that their recall helps me in trying to explain the way I work in mime, which is largely through sense of *touch*.

To me, sense of touch is not confined to physical contact with objects. There is the touch transmitted by sight of something — an electric communication with memory; the touch of an idea — or that touch which is the feel of space. Awareness and sense of touch are, to me, synonymous.


## Aside: The Air is a Solid

I have no way of knowing how other performers effect projection of their idea — or character — but for me this is a tactile thing, which I shall endeavor to explain.

I have heard, here and there, of a theory that performers must develop a sense of freedom in space. That is, they must feel unhampered by a fearful sense of being stranded, alone, in a strange void, the void of the stage itself, which extends out into the space occupied by the audience.

My own feeling about space is quite the opposite. To me, the air is a solid, but an elastic solid, comparable to the clay

58

prepared by the modeler before he begins his work. It is a resilient medium, on which I can imprint my meaning; and beyond that, it has curious electric properties — it carries the intention of this imprint outward, in a kind of telegraphic code — in a message to myself as the entire audience from myself as the instrument of the character performed.

To me, this is no obscure, esoteric theory, but tangible reality.

I must try to clarify this by saying that, as mime, and apart from the character, I am a dual personality. That is, I exist both as the instrument through which the character reveals him-her-or-itself and as the one and only audience beyond the footlights. It is to me, as alter ego, that the character reveals himself. That others are present is only incidental, and their responses are no more than repercussions resulting from the spark of communication between the character and myself.

When I, acting as the physical instrument through which the character reveals himself, make a gesture — any movement, even a glance or a smile — I have a tactile sense of its engraving an indelible imprint on the air, no matter how fleeting the impulse which sends it forth.

This is not so abstruse as it may first seem, for to everyone, images of movements and their meanings remain in memory long after they have transpired. We remember the flight of a bird long after it has disappeared from sight. Thus to me the air is not space, but a tangible and sympathetic medium in which to imprint the image of my imagination — an image which I hope the beholder will continue to experience in memory just as the voyager after his trip experiences as though still present the color and sparkle of the sea, the feeling of its surges, and the thoughts brought on by speculation on the contents of its fearsome depths.

Let me hasten to add that I do not consider my perception, as audience to the character, greater than that of other viewers; but I do assume that whatever fascinates me about the aspects of any character I perform may arouse interest in them. I am totally devoid of any talent for conjecturing what may please an audience and can only, like Carmen, sing to please myself.

## Log: Ninth Session

Am reconciled to a program directed toward the awakening of their physical sensibilities into collaboration with whatever images occur to them — with a view toward clearing the sluggish obstructions between mind and matter.

Began by asking them to respond, through finger-tip intelligence, to the entire effect of heat and cold. Next had them imagine the handling of familiar objects — such as a cigarette being taken from a pack and lighted. Their look of amazement at the fallibility of their sense-memory was reward for proposing so simple an exercise. To emphasize to them their insensitivity to touch, had them perform, in imagination, other familiar tasks — tying a knot, taking off a wet raincoat, etc.

As these were problems which they were unlikely to encounter as actors, it seemed to me a good idea to provide an exercise wherein the tactile quality of a gesture was combined with the spoken word.

Remembered a few lines from Dryden where gesture could be used compatibly with words.

Look 'round our world
    Behold the chain of love
Uniting all below
And all above.

Gave them a brief synopsis of the advent of the literary theatre, stemming from Molière; and suggested that these lines be performed as though spoken, with gestures, by a poet in an eighteenth-century drawing room. Release from the imposed stricture of performing in silence was welcomed, although they soon found that relating of gesture to words presented unexpected problems. The most obvious problem was to avoid deflecting the meaning of the lines by erratic movements. More subtle, but far more challenging was the problem of presenting simultaneously a view of the period and place in which the action was set, and — in balance with the milieu being created — an individual character, true to its own peculiar impulses and personality. This led to an exposition of the difference between manner and manners.

### Manner and Manners

Manner and manners, while not synonymous, both have to do with the outward way in which we do things.

Everyone has a manner individual to himself, a manner which, together with physical appearance, makes him instantly recognizable to others. His manner is the natural result of his upbringing, mental powers, age, physical state etc., all of which combine to produce this person's unique responses, both when he is alone and when he is in the company of others. Manner, in other words, is simply the way one responds physically to any experience and it cannot fail to indicate one's point of view toward the circumstances of life.

In mime, as in literature, creation of character is not literal transference of one's own manner of behavior. To transfer literally is to deprive the character of its own personality and to make of it a figure tantamount to a dummy, painted, dressed,

61

and arranged to simulate reality, as are those waxen figures in Madame Tussaud's Museum.

Invention of character is a curious transmigration whereby through imagination abetted by historical knowledge and personal experience we bring a creature to life and in doing so are astonished to discover ourselves at one with it — but ourselves stripped of our own manner and mannerisms.

Since this creature owes his life to the understanding of his inventor, it is inevitable that its manner is accented by its creator's point of view. It is this point of view in his work which reveals the perception of the mime-as-artist.

The mime may choose to present his character with sympathy or in a critical light, by accenting subtleties of manner which reveal unselfishness on the one hand or unwarranted self-pity on the other.

The mime draws character with gesture and movement; the painter draws character with the sweep of the brush.

I think it was Samuel Butler who said that every portrait is a self-portrait of the artist, but by this he did not mean that the painter literally ascribed his own characteristics to his figure. In any portraiture, and mime is an art of portraiture, no matter how abstractly or concretely the subject may be presented, it is the point of view of the artist that brings it to life.

Lucian summarized brilliantly the aim of the mime:

> You will find that his is no easy profession, not lightly to be undertaken; requiring as it does, the highest standard of culture . . . and involving a knowledge of music not only, but of rhythm and metre . . . the exposition of human character and human passion claims a share of its attention. Nor can it dispense with the painter's and sculptor's art . . . in its close observance of the harmonious proportions that these teach. But above all, Mnemosyne and her daughter Polyphemia, must be propitiated by an art that would re-

62

*"Aphrodisiac — Green Hour"*

member all things. The pantomime must know all "that is, that was, that shall be"; nothing must escape his ready memory. Faithfully to represent his subject, adequately to express his own conception, to make plain all that might be obscure — these are the first essentials of mime.

To accomplish this the mime does not present a representation of himself but of an idea-image. For this exposition he uses recognizable symbols.

The underlying natural manner of the character is accentuated by his mannerisms. These, broadly speaking, fall into two categories: those which are unconscious nervous habits of movement and those which are adopted in public, the latter formed by his image of himself in the company of others. These mannerisms may at first be assumed and later become part of his unconscious manner.

As I try to formulate the distinction between these two forms of mannerism I am conscious, for the first time, of an example of the former kind in myself. In a pause of choosing a word or phrase while typing, I either hold my hands suspended over the keys after the impact of the last one struck, or, in longer reflection, I clasp my hands in a kind of gesture of desperation while seeking for a way to continue. In writing by hand I spend this interval making marginal drawings, usually geometric designs. Mannerisms characteristic of me in private.

I cannot recall any public-personal mannerisms except two, which I may also indulge in while alone. One, which the group recognizes, is that of automatically brushing aside my bangs before speaking, a gesture which I suppose results from the attempt to clarify a thought — a brushing away of cobwebs. The other is a mannerism of slowing down in entering any place, or in answering the telephone when I am uncertain what is to be faced. But this last, I believe, is not individual to me.

*Manners*, generally speaking, are the conformities or non-conformities to social behavior, and are a matter of personal choice — except in cases where ignorance makes a person unaware of a kind of behavior beyond his own natural manner; or where he is oblivious to the presence of anyone but himself.

Montaigne in his essay on the education of children outlines one rule for *good* manners which can be extended in wider context to the portrayal of character:

Any strangeness and peculiarity in our conduct and way is to be avoided as inimical to social intercourse and *unnattural*.

It is an excellent rule for the performer to keep in mind. The mimist must be personally inconspicuous — he must avoid inflicting his own mannerisms onto the character he is portraying; if he fails, it will have the deadly result of making his character appear only a mimist in charade.

We come now to *etiquette*, which has to do with familiarity with the social forms of any stratum of society. This requires not only research into what was proper etiquette in a certain period, but also perception of the logic behind etiquettes.

The mime, as a citizen of the world, past or present, must be cognizant of whatever stratum of society involves his character; for the character's attitude toward the etiquette of that social stratum is instrumental in portraying his individuality.

In *First Person Plural* I endeavored to explain briefly my own approach to the past:

History has many appearances, detours and blind alleys. These appearances have many forms and one can easily lose one's way. One is obliged, like Theseus, to take· a thread into the labyrinths of history, and to weave that thread with what one finds. An age is like a vain man or woman in that it puts on masks and mascara to enhance itself. If you look at an age as you look at an artificed woman, or man, you invariably see the old familiar face of humanity beneath.

Leonardo said: "In rivers the waters that you touch is the last of what has passed and the first of which comes; so with time present."*

The mime feels at home in any time or place and, forgetful of himself, accommodates himself to its demands.

## *Log: Tenth Session*

Today, at one point in the play, noticed one of the players acting in a peculiar manner; his face had an abstracted expression and the use of his property was broken by what I can only call blank seconds or missed beats.

I am not always as patient as I wish, and I called out to him "*What* are you doing?"

Startled at the interruption, he looked at me as though surprised at my obtuseness and replied, with dignity, "I'm justifying."

"Not here — not here!" I answered more sharply than I should have, and while there were a few appreciative laughs, there came from other players who had had previous dramatic training a shocked silence of consternation which told me that I had committed a sacrilege.

I explained that I considered what we were doing a performance and that if "justification" was to be discovered it was to be discovered in private.

This bald statement required elaboration, as this student and most of the others were clearly puzzled. Said the following:

* From *First Person Plural*, by Angna Enters, with illustrations by the author. Copyright © 1937, 1965 by Angna Enters. New York, Stackpole Sons, 1937.

While the theory of justifying the behavior of a character to make it compatible with one's own has some validity, in practice, when literally applied, it often defeats its own purpose.

The understanding that the effect of an experience on another bears some relation to oneself certainly does not mean that the characters whom we invent — or those presented by the playwright — respond exactly as we do to the same experience.

The effect of any experience varies with each individual — real or imagined. Were this not true, as I may have said in another connection, all human beings would be identical in their responses.

It is only natural that on first acquaintance with our characters, just as in meeting any stranger, we seek a fundamental basis for communication; for no one can understand another except through personal experience, in which we identify with or relate to another on the basis of our common element of humanity.

But experience cautions us against merely identifying our own reactions with those of others, for it teaches the endless dissimilarities as well as the similarities among people. For the mime it is a grave error to assume that the various characters he is called upon to portray will follow his own line of demeanor in comparable circumstances.

It is of course true that all human beings have the same basic human emotions, and for this reason we can recognize ourselves in each other, even though the actual reactions differ by degrees with the individual. Hence, as viewers in the theatre, we may laugh at some quizzical smile or glance by a char-

acter in a play because in it is reflected some comparable behavior of our own — in a quite dissimilar circumstance. So in
mime do we enlarge and embroider our memories in working
on our characters, inventing circumstances which our memories stimulate, but with the imperative that it be done within
the scope of their reason, not ours.

The relationship between the performer and his character
is a delicate one, for, in mime, the performer is the abnegating
lover who permits his character as much freedom as possible
without consciously imposing on it the stamp of his own personality.

In viewing those performances where the theory of justification rides rampant, I find myself distracted by the imposi-
tion of this extra consideration, for it not only conceals the
erratic responses one expects from the character as a separate
individual, but it also causes a time lag, however infinitesimal,
in the natural line of the character's thoughts and reactions.
To my eye, this is as blatant as if a pianist were to hesitate in
a performance to calculate the tone of each note or phrase before striking it.

I find that I learn more about myself from my characters
than they do from me; that their impulses are often contrary
to my own in a like situation, and that they often surprise me
in their reactions; and I marvel, almost like a bystander, at
their trueness to themselves. But then, I am not entranced with
my own nature or reactions — I find I have many faults — and
I have no wish to inflict these on imagined characters.

Like others who work in the arts, I get invitations from
professional psychiatrists asking me to confess in their presence the way I work. I evade such inquisitions with the face-
tious excuse that I do not wish to tamper with my inhibitions,

for I consider them the fertilizer of whatever images I have. Frankly, I am afraid of blunting my intuition, and prefer to let it ferment with as little interference from reason as possible: for reason is a strong contestant and enters of its own free will to judge and organize intuition.

No doubt this is a romantic and unpopular view to the scientific mind, but right or wrong, I find it best to adhere to my own superstitions. Reasoned probings, I grant, might lead to better compatibility with myself in personal life, but I prefer to suffer a few discomforts rather than interfere with the effluvium of the imagination, lest it evaporate.

In private contemplation one may try to fathom the behavior of an image and whilst so doing, give consideration to one's own physical reactions. But to me, this is rather like a diver, perched on a springboard, gathering his forces and at the same time seeing himself reflected in the still water beneath. The moment he pierces the water his own image is dispersed and he must accommodate himself to this element as best he can.

Spending a life devoted to working in the arts is a form of madness for which the only cure is death, or the alternative — to become completely reasonable — which in so far as one's work is concerned, is far worse.


## Aside: A One-sided Love Affair

The relationship between the performer and his character is as delicate as that between two human beings of whom one, easily offended, must be treated with utmost sympathetic understanding lest the bond disappear. It is a one-sided love relationship in which the performer is the lover of a self-centered, demanding mistress. The moment the lover ventures to suggest that he too is an individual entitled to consideration and is even the master, she, the image, vanishes.

There are those love exhibitions carried on in public where the love affair is that of the performer with himself. Such persons are what might be termed "personality performers" — performers to whom the character is no more than a robe with which to enhance themselves.

This exhibitionism has legitimate place in the manifold realm of entertainment, and it does entrance some members of an audience, who see in the performer an enviable freedom of self-expression for which they themselves long but which they can experience only through vicarious means. For them, watching a performer's exhibitionism is a kind of pleasurable cathartic.

But mime does not afford the audience this particular kind of release. It offers instead a more, or at least an equally intensive pleasure, to which one could apply George Bernard Shaw's phrase "the ecstasy of the mind."

And anyway, there is no such thing as THE audience, for an audience is but a congregation of persons gathered with expectations of viewing one or another type of performance. The audience comes with different outlooks to witness a production of Shakespeare, a tap dancer, a musical comedy, a night-club performer, or a play in the contemporary idiom.

It adjusts its viewpoint to the occasion. It will adjust its viewpoint in watching mime.

The mime-as-actor does the best he can to cajole the image of his invention into functioning as an independent entity; and concentrating on this precludes concern with other viewers

71

as individuals with their own points of view. A performer is more likely to satisfy an audience if he can communicate his intimate understanding of his protagonist (the character) rather than indicate his concern for the viewers. That is wasted effort: it succeeds only in distracting the audience and in blurring his own perception of the character.

## Aside: Hydra

We are at the mercy of dictations from an inexplicable phenomenon called the mind.

This omnific miracle controlling our thoughts and actions is not a machine responding identically to identical stimuli, but is a double-headed Hydra, one head of which is named Intuition, the other, Reason.

These unidentical twins, two bickering devils, work in harmony only sporadically, for each, jealous of its power, claims credit for our virtues and blames the other for our vices.

Nature, while burdening us with this double-headed monster, delights perversely in not endowing either with complete loyalty. Each can play us false and they often do when we try to court them separately. They seem to delight in playing a coquettish game of hide-and-seek when we endeavor to summon their separate aids.

Only when they have succeeded in reducing us to a state of helplessness do these two fiends, unexpectedly, collaborate to strike and ignite an illuminating flash, which reveals the path to our goal.

I feel myself no more than an instrument, a helpless Trilby, mesmerized by the aberrations of this contrary creature to which I can only abandon myself in the hope that their battles will resolve into a love union in which they will conceive a work of art.

## Aside: Deja Vue

Deja vue — that already seen — the disturbing sense which overcomes one at times in a foreign territory of having been there before and known it intimately; not only in one's own time but also in some former life; what occurs is tactile recognition of a former experience. Reason rejects such unreason with little effect, even if one is disinclined toward mystical explanations.

I do not believe that this persistent sense is individual to me, and I simply use it, whenever it occurs, for whatever it may contribute to my work. When I do think of it at all, which is rarely, I lay it to that inexplicable faculty of the mind which the psychologists call "sense memory" or "association of ideas." Whatever it is, it exists; and I do not trouble myself with self-investigations as to its source. I am grateful for any illuminating flash which makes me at home with the past and would not dream of fooling with scientific explanations. Deja vue is not a faculty to be summoned at will. It occurs in its own good time, when least expected.

When it does happen, as many know, the experience is unsettling.

Many years ago, the day before leaving Paris, I had gone to get some paints at Sennlier's on the Left Bank, and wishing to take a last look at a few particular paintings in the Louvre, I crossed over to walk up along the river to the main entrance to the museum. I had not been acquainted with the vast interior of the palace beyond the galleries arrived at by way of this entrance. I came to a portal which led into a cobble courtyard, and while I was not attracted to the ordeal of walking on its stones, as the day was burning hot, I thought I could find a shortcut to my destination if I did walk across. There wasn't a large public door, as I hoped to find, but only a small open doorway through which I spied narrow, winding steps. Relieved from the heat in the dank coolness, and adjusting my eyes to the darkness of the interior, I decided to see whether the steps would lead me to my objective.

As I began my ascent, the worn old stones felt familiar to my feet and a curious change overtook my body. My fashionable, short-skirted silk suit was insidiously replaced by a heavy, tight-bodiced robe, and beneath the thick folds of its long skirt my knees strained against the weight as I climbed, tread by tread. My breathing changed, adjusting to this strain.

"This is ridiculous," I told myself, with a feeling of panic, and tried for reassurance to feel my thighs under the silk of the suit. My arms, however, would not stretch straight down, but instead curved at the elbow — because of the thick, full sleeves of the bodice; and when my finger tips did touch the skirt, they felt velvet.

Frightened and wary, I thought, "Keep calm until you reach the top, you will come to." I thought of myself as "you" not "I." I arrived at the top and went into a narrow corridor which eventually led into a gallery of early nineteenth-century portraits. I recognized the portraits — slowly — but seeing something I recognized released me only partially from the spell. Shaken, I came at last to the room of the familiar paint-

74

ings I had expressly wanted to see, but they seemed foreign because of the sense of having come from the past.

A year or two later, I happened upon a book which had to do with the architecture of the Louvre. I came to a picture of the steps I had climbed with such disturbing effects. I found that they were called the Henry IV steps, built for access to the apartments of his mistress!

I do not ascribe my experience to extrasensory perception but lay it to subconscious memory of my readings. (Oddly enough, what had been retained more consciously in so far as the Louvre was concerned was an account of the Saint Bartholomew Massacre, which the royal family had viewed from the windows in the opposite wing.)

My earliest travels abroad began in 1928, the year of my London theatre debut, before the influx of foreign films in America and before television. Hence except for sketchy newsreels I had no way of viewing foreign scenes. But one of the surprises in travel was that I was surprised so little; and I was puzzled that so many places seemed so familiar.

No one had prepared me on what to expect upon my first arrival in Paris, which took place late on a drizzling, misty night. Yet nothing was strange — beginning with the boat train from Calais, continuing through the confusion at the station, the taxi ride through winding streets to the hotel, the crimson, plush, flower-papered, brass-steaded bedroom, and the first meeting with the *femme de chambre* — all were familiar. Was it Balzac or Maupassant or Degas or Lautrec or Baudelaire or Verlaine who prepared me for this? Had I already seen Monet's painting of the train smoking into the Gare St. Lazare?

Whatever it was, so it is when I read of the life and customs of the past. All seem present and familiar.

75

In *First Person Plural* I wrote: "Travel for me is a kind of search for something I am not seeking but something which when I find it, seems to have been with me all the time."

Watching a play, one can tell by intuition rather than reason whether the player arrives at his portrayal of a character by theoretical planning or by *deja vue*.

## Aside: Odalisque

*From a notebook: Inception of "Odalisque" — 1927*

Théophile Gautier wrote: "Spanish dancing girls have not the finish, perfect correctness and grand style of Frenchwomen, but, in my opinion, they far surpass them in grace and charm; they work very little, and do not go in for those terrible exercises in flexibility which make a dancing class like a torture chamber, so they escape that leanness, like that of a horse in training, which gives our ballets such a macabre and anatomical touch; they preserve the rounded contours of their sex; they look like women dancing, not dancing-women, which is quite a different thing."

Good! Explains one reason why I was not moved by St. D., found her "Nautch Dance" only a well-performed routine. No sex. Was told sometime later by one of her pupils that she theorizes it as a religious dance without sexual connotation. The trouble with dancers is that they all move around too much — are continually displaying their technique! Another thing about that performance which was disturbing was the obvious manipulation of all those draperies. All too calculated, to my taste. Gautier, Guys, Loti, Delacroix, Renoir — all had a *nostalgie du*

76

*Maroc. Haremlik* life. What do I think of when I think of Morocco and Turkey — in addition to Guys' drawings of the Crimean War? Not dancers. *Haremlik life* — closed in — heat — droning flies — stuffy draperies — shutters to keep out the hot afternoon sun — siestas, such as we took in Spain just across. Granada — the women's quarters in the Alhambra. Some day we must cross the Straits. How did those women spend their time, those odalisques? Sitting, gossiping, eating sweetmeats, sleeping during the hot hours? In childish play?

How could one show such a woman? Asleep on a couch? One cannot show only someone asleep, like a *tableau vivant*.

Up and down with the curtain!

There she is, asleep, on a couch rumpled from the sticky heat — turned away toward a draped screen, her head hidden — buttocks mostly in view, weight of her hips indenting the soft couch. A shaft of sunlight strikes and half-awakens her; hot, she turns lazily and readjusts herself to a fresher position, at the same time shoving her hair up over the pillow to cool her moist neck. She stretches, still drowsy, remembers the dance movements (*danse du ventre*) which entrance her lord. Thoughts of love. Music? That Turkish air in the collection I found in Paris — but must be played as though strummed lazily on a stringed instrument — NOT a piano! It needs an accent. What about her having fallen asleep with a pair of finger cymbals on one hand? Good! The ones made by that old man in Paris which I could not resist buying. The sound excites her and brings her to life for a few moments; she enjoys the voluptuous feel of her hand on her cheek, throat, and breasts — it arouses her senses — but this passes and she relaxes again into sleep.

But I am too pale for her lush rosiness — also must simulate more flesh to my body in the movements. A white pillow

77

on top of colored cushions will raise my head to view, and the white will make my face darker. If I dye China silk in Spanish saffron, its yellow will darken my face too. This for the blouse — and over it, a gold-embroidered red-velvet bolero. The trousers? Full — that pomegranate and white striped cotton with roses that I bought in Spain — copy of an old cotton fabric. Too much red and white — paint in splashes here and there, with deep turquoise dye . . . That maroon velvet drape can cover the couch — an Oriental rug over the screen . . . for the cushions, that green tinsel, and black striped material in the fabric trunk — and also another of the same but with the red stripes. Let the green cushion lie on the floor at the foot of the couch — as if fallen off. White cotton stockings, slipping down — one Moroccan slipper has fallen off — those bought from the Algerian street vendor in Paris . . . All those items bought here and there without purpose have a purpose!

Will anyone but myself be interested in watching such sustained laziness? I am — it is worth a try.

Stay away from "the Art of the Dance!"


*Postscript to "Odalisque"*

As in painting or writing, I find it impossible in the theatre to contrive anything for appeal to an audience. I work on ideas that interest me and take a chance that these may interest others. If they do not, I assume that I have been unable to communicate my idea. Sometimes such a failure seems to me unreasonable imperceptiveness in the viewer, but always it causes re-examination of the work. More often than not, I have found that if I have a firm and undeviating conception of an idea, it is communicated to others. Although I work without words and in many styles of movement dictated by the demands of

78

"Odalisque"

the idea, it has often happened that people who have seen me perform have subsequently said to me, "I *heard* you" in such or such a place, and look at me, amazed, when reminded that I never speak.

In the case of "Odalisque," no one could have been more astonished than myself at its reception, for I had been convinced to the moment of its first presentation that no one but myself would be interested. It has, however, remained one of the classics of my repertoire, testimony to the unpredictable interests of audiences. Sometimes, luckily not often, characters have failed to meet what I was certain would be the expected response. Later, discomposed by their failure, I have sought to revise them for clearer projection. This rarely works, and they are at last abandoned and replaced by newer works; but they persist in remaining clear to me, in their original image. Sometimes they reappear in their essence but in entirely different guise and situation — and are accepted by the viewers.

About "Odalisque": Several years after its first performance, I did visit Morocco and was guest in a harem, from which I came away relieved to be confirmed in what had been no more than a *deja vue* of its life. The only change made was a pictorial one — replacement of the Oriental rug over the screen by a sheer, aged linen drape, with an over-all pattern woven in gold threads, acquired in Tetuan — a drape which still serves, as does the original costume; for I can never substitute anything beyond the conception of the character as it first appears to me. This, as can well be imagined, poses a problem in retaining characters in their original image when the costume is worn out. For I am reluctant to replace the original with a copy.

81

## Log: Eleventh Session

*Breathing*

In the warm-up today, in order to afford them practice in unifying gesture, movement, and thought, gave them a descriptive line from a classical play to be performed in mime alone. To contain it within a definite time limit, played for them a few lines of music (Rameau — never mind the neo-classical aspect!) which they were to retain in memory. After a few tries they did manage to do this, but their culminating gesture lacked authority. This is a characteristic of their work to be rectified.

Watching them, it suddenly struck me that they do not know how to breathe!

Rehearsed in mind what happens to me when I performed, and remembered this: My own rhythm of breathing and pulse changes into that of each character. After the rush of each costume change, while in the wings, or on stage, waiting for the rise of the curtain, that last thing I do is to expel the breath from the rush, and with the rise of the curtain take a long, slow breath, the exhalation of which propels me into the rhythm of the breathing of the character. To calculate this, had to relive that moment in imagination, and found that this happens automatically.

In my own case the transformation must take quickly, because of the costume changes, during which period there is the added preoccupation of worry whether the stage crew will have the stage in the expected order of properties and lights — something with which players need not ordinarily be concerned. But now, thinking of it, I wonder whether this transformation does not begin back in the dressing room and not just before the curtain; while I change I already hear the background music which will accompany the next character, even if I am distracted with other thoughts. In any case, with this preparation, once the curtain is up, the character breathes according to its own demands.

82

Remember that once at a particularly harried moment I wondered why I was short of breath after making my entrance, and realized that my breathing was unnatural for the character. With a deep inhalation, I made the adjustment from my rhythm into its, and found the character at ease with itself. A technical solution which has proved invaluable. It was this circumstance that first made me aware that normally the figures of my theatre have pulses and rhythms of breathing quite different from mine and from those of one another.

This was confirmed when I experimented in dictating the manner in which they were to breathe in the performance of this simple exercise. As they performed it singly, while the others watched along with me, the effect was electric. How much they will retain of this experience and how they apply it remain to be seen.

I had intended that we would now go into the play, but one of the players, a singer about to make her debut as Rosina in *The Marriage of Figaro*, asked for help in a problem in breathing with which the director had given no aid.

The difficulty was this: Rosina was required, in one scene, to enter on the run and throw open the shutters of a window upstage right of center, then run left, peer offstage to see whether she was alone, circle back to upstage center, and come directly down, prepared to sing her aria. All this direction, she found, left her breathless.

Since I cannot ask of them something I cannot do myself, experimented a few times and found this solution:

A deep, slow breath before entrance — hold it while running to the window (for suspense) — exhale it in the gesture of throwing open the shutter.

Inhale while rushing to next window.

Exhale in throwing open second shutter.

Inhale while running to peer out doorway left.

Hold breath while peering (suspense).

Now, relieved at being alone, exhale slowly while circling quickly to place, upstage center, where, in turning front, take a short inhale-exhale.

Now, facing front, while walking straight down to sing, take a long, slow inhale to prepare for immediate beginning of aria.

Although I do not speak or sing, this seemed to me natural to a character in such a circumstance. She tried it and found that it worked, as she said, "like a charm." As the group and I watched her rehearse, it seemed natural and not at all contrived, as indeed it had been.

## Log: Twelfth Session

Proposed that we take time out from the play to solve a single problem in a variety of manners, an idea heartily received. Thought that this might be easier for them and also more profitable to them as actors were they given some descriptive line to speak, a suggestion which relieved them of their fear of performing in silence.

Offered the first line which came to mind as a possibility for a scene that could be done with or without words: "A rose by any other name would smell as sweet." The only restriction was that the line be taken out of its Shakespearean context and used solely as a source for improvisation.

Luckily, we discovered among the properties an artificial rose, short-stemmed and battered, which we placed in a glass on a small table, center stage. Each player was required to follow the same blocking: enter left, see the rose, respond to its presence, and exit opposite. Each scene was to have dramatic unity.

It was agreed that no comment would be made by anyone until all had finished. What happened was this: Each player entered so well-prepared with a preconceived reaction to the rose and came over to it so directly that the scene was robbed of the dramatic element of the *discovery* of the flower. Everything they did with it was also too obviously precalculated.

84

The last player was a young woman, called at the end because she was the most timid and I wished her to have time to observe the others and gather courage. This did profit her, for she did seem to come upon the rose unexpectedly and displayed a warmer relationship to it than had the others, who had given it a somewhat cavalier treatment.

Except for her, from whom I had been prepared to expect the least, no one recognized the flower as a living thing or considered any of its characteristic properties.

Told them that other than she they had been mainly concerned with *what* to do, and that in mime, in the use of properties, it is not as important *what* is done as *how*, for it is this which reveals the character.

Went on to elaborate on the subject of properties.

### Properties

Performers too often view objects with which they must deal, and, at times, even their gestures, as "business." To me, "business" is a horrid word, for it implies contrived effects, either in gesture or in the use of objects.

To illustrate my meaning in relation to gesture: A young actor who had just had his first important role was brought to visit me. Intending a compliment, he said, "I used a piece of business with the eyes that you do in 'Boy Cardinal'." That he believed that a glance or gesture could be transplanted with full effect told me that he was probably only a stock actor. I think that my suspicion was not far wrong, for although he subsequently had several fine opportunities in roles, nothing came of them, and he has disappeared from the theatre scene.

BUSINESS DOES NOT MAKE THE CHARACTER — THE CHARACTER MAKES ITS OWN BUSINESS.

The character of our invention does not exist in a vacuum, any more than does any human being. He lives in his world, removed from one's own in time, place, and condition. In his world he has contact not only with persons but with objects.

In the theatre, these objects, movable or immovable, are named "properties" for the convenience of the stage crew, whose job it is to see that they are in place on the scene, or ready to be taken up and carried on by the player.

One of the means by which character is revealed is through intimation of his relationship to these objects. They may be real, imaginary, or abstract symbol devices of the set designer, but to the character they must have definite meaning.

There are brilliant exponents of the stylized French school of mime who specialize in the delineation of imaginary objects. I recall one such mime who plays on a nonexistent keyboard with such extraordinary facility that the piano is conjured up into reality for the audience. But such a feat requires that the performer be an experienced musician — that he have a tactile memory of the instrument, even to the extent of knowing the tension in the fingertips needed to create dynamics: this is a highly specialized form of mime.

In a play, actors-as-mimes rarely have the time to impress their audience with this technical proficiency; it must be accomplished subversively, without drawing attention.

In mime, with or without words, there is no such thing as an inanimate object any more than there is in life. A door to be opened or shut, a rock against which one stumbles, the sharp corner of a table on which one may bruise oneself, all are living objects. A chair receives us as a familiar friend or as an unwelcome stranger.

A rose has properties with which we are all familiar. It is not only a fragrant flower, but it has a thorned stem. In mime, our fingers feel this hazard, although we may not have to take obvious note of it — unless obvious note is required for some

86

comic or dramatic purpose — lest it distract from the central line of intention. Nevertheless, the character is aware of the presence of thorns, and this affects his sense of touch. In mime, any insincerities or evasions of a character in relation to the properties with which he must deal are magnified in both the intuitive and the reasoning mind of the viewer.

Both as a performer and as a member of audiences, I have discovered a curious fact: that the space between the stage and the audience is a magnifying glass. In nature, details diminish according to the law of perspective, a law followed by landscape painters from the primitives to Cezanne. In the theatre, the opposite is true. Nothing which happens on the stage, however far up, escapes the eye of the audience. It is literalminded, and it sees only what is before it and hears only what it is told. It has a contrary eye, inclined to magnify what a player may believe an insignificant detail. It is aware that a set is painted to only resemble reality and that objects are spurious — unless the performer dissuades it from such thoughts through his acceptance of the objects as realities.

He must endow these shams with qualities supplied by his imagination, just as a child pushing a row of blocks across a floor will scream, convinced that it is true, "Choo-choo-choo — get out of the way, here comes the train!" And what adult will not have an image of an onrushing train while indulging the child's fantasy?

A theatre production may be designed in a style in which abstract forms replace representational objects: in which the player is called to accept a few steps or an ovoid object as a symbol of a mountain to be climbed, or to use a yardstick as an umbrella. Any indication by the player that such objects are merely substitutions for reality, unless this is the intent, denies the audience *their* willingness to collaborate in a fantasy. We have all been deflected from such acceptance of a scene because it was evident that the actor or dancer did not with imagination seriously accept the properties as realities and not shams.

I have always used all three kinds of properties — realistic, symbolic, and imagined — depending on the style in which the number is performed. More often than not I use recognizable properties, for the simple reason that I wish to conceal my technical capabilities from the audience, for their fuller concentration on the character and for pictorial reasons.

As I do not travel with any properties except for a few small items which can be packed in the costume trunks, I must rely on each theatre to supply me with an approximation of what is required. However makeshift these often are, in performance they have a way of becoming normal to the character, for I see them not as they are, but as they should be.

They have intimate meaning to the character, just as I at home see the furnishings not only as they appear in actuality, but as living objects which persist in recalling their past to my mind. Whilst in some thought quite apart, I find myself looking at some table, chair, or chest — something — and without detracting from my primary preoccupation, it conjures up its past and the circumstances under which it came into my possession, or impresses me with its physical aspect. So does this happen, to a degree, in the theatre; were this not true, it would be difficult for me to accommodate myself to each otherwise foreign object.

# Log: Thirteenth Session

### The Face

In class, as at a play, I am drawn to watch the faces of the performers. It is there that the meanings of their words and the shades of their thoughts are communicated.

Everyone, at times, presents a mask of one kind or another before the world, a guard behind which we at times strive to conceal our thoughts; one which often deceives no one but ourselves.

The faces of these players while performing their parts in the play are expressionless masks because they are uncertain, they fear to give way to intuition lest it be in error.

Told them what I saw, and they confessed that their faces felt constrained. Told them that this, too, was a sign of self-consciousness, and for their benefit tried to recall the state of my face when I perform. I can tell from the way my face feels even more than my body, how ready I am for performance. It feels alive and tingles, ready to respond to thoughts and mood. I never calculate these reactions, they happen. I never enforce accents of my own upon those of the character for this would throw it into the realm of caricature. It is true that the tempi and breadth of expressions vary, depending on the distance to which they must be projected, as does the tone of one's voice in speaking to someone far or near. But the quality remains unchanged.

Someone asked about my change of makeup from one number to another, and they were surprised when I said that I do not change makeup during a performance, for they had assumed that this took place. Explained that the necessary rapidity of costume changes gave no time for makeup revisions.

The truth is that when I first began in the theatre it never occurred to me to use any makeup beyond that necessary to make my eyes and mouth visible to the audience. I took it for granted that the characters performed would draw their own images through the responses of my face. I knew nothing of the art of makeup and used only what seemed necessary. What was expedient to avoid prolonged intervals for costume change. My face has no extreme variations in its modelling, and thus a thin foundation, the same color as my skin, just enough to hold the outlining of my eyes, and lip rouge, was used. I did not use mascara for I found that in the heat of the performance, if I closed my eyes, it left a smudge which had to be repaired while changing. I did, however, darken my eyebrows a trifle. Now, in my increasing years I still use the same makeup, but even a thinner base, less than many women do in ordinary life, and I have almost dispensed entirely with powder unless the climate is very hot. Every performer must find the makeup most congenial to the contours of his face and, of course, in the case of those who play a single character, one revelatory of it. My style of makeup suits my needs perfectly. I dislike the stiffening feel of a thick foundation; I prefer to feel my face as free on the stage as in ordinary life. For my purpose I like as little interference with the living tissue as possible, and my makeup was devised to make of my face a breathing mask.

This explanation led to a question of what is known as "dead pan" performing.

The term "dead pan" is a misnomer born of a convention of a flat white or pale makeup which makes the face appear a mask. But despite the single color which surfaces the face of such performers, it is far from expressionless although the impression of thoughts on its surface must be more consciously simplified and exaggerated to penetrate through the thick grease paint; an adjustment in projection which comes only through experience.

Mime is performed, too, with actual masks, as in stylized productions of classical plays or in the Noh drama of Japan. Technically, the expressions of the face which are left to the imagination of the audience, are controlled entirely by the actions of the neck muscles aided by gestures of the hands.

Any style of makeup is legitimate in the theatre, as is any

style of performing, so long as it serves its purpose. And so far as the face is concerned, all that is necessary is that the player be sensitive to its nervous reactions and use them with discretion so that they do not run wild.

The face is a sun whose brilliance radiates out from the heat of its core in the form of reflected thought and intuition.

To break through the mask of their personal reserve and sensitize them to their faces gave them this exercise: Had them, very slowly, begin a smile and gradually broaden it until it broke naturally into a free laugh. This would naturally throw back their heads. I was careful to explain that such a free action would not be true to every character or in every circumstance. That this was an exercise in an extreme instance. From there they were asked to slowly diminish the laugh into a smile, which would end in a sombre thought-mood.

They were taken aback to find how difficult this was for them to perform (they are often unsettled by the effect of our exercises) because of the tenseness of their natural habits. The muscles of their lips and faces were stiffer than they had thought. Their intellects and inhibitions get in the way of their instinctive reactions. At least, in public.

Their faces ached but their eyes were brighter and their lips more sensitive. Had them then taste, in imagination, sweet and bitter, cold and burning hot, with aftereffects of these sensations to show on their faces. A primitive exercise! Had them give quick, free smiles and ones sceptical or forced. Then had them say things to each other and respond with their faces. Once given such clues they enjoy inventing exchanges with each other.

What I saw when we finished was that their faces were more alert — more, perhaps, than they realized, and I can only hope that this sensitivity is retained.

## The Eyes

Leonardo da Vinci: "The eyes are the mirror of the soul."

Told them today that their eyes are lazy, that they *look* but do not *see*.

Demonstrated how sightless their eyes had appeared to me by performing as they had the short dramatic passage which had led me to discover their faulty breathing.

In this passage, the ultimate point of the last gesture should have been punctuated by having the eyes carry to a definite, distant point. Normally, this would happen automatically. But they had performed like students, obeying literally the director's instructions as to scene duration and rhythm, and forgetting to think of the meaning of the scene. This was relayed by the lack of focus in their eyes, which they were not equipped to cope with technically.

Then performed it again as it could have been done so that the gesture gained meaning through the *seeing* of the distant point. They grasped this graphic illustration, and we rehearsed the exercise again with notable improvements. They also found that the fact that they "saw" the imaginary distant point stimulated a feeling of greater authenticity in the gesture.

I had noted that, in their scenes in the play, direct looks at anyone or anything were often broken by blinking. Of course blinking is an automatic nervous release of the eye muscles natural to everyone; but it is also indicative of indecision in thought or mood. It can be distracting, as it is to me at times watching television players. In mime in any form, blinking at inopportune moments hinders or breaks that line of intention which the audience seeks to follow. It is a natural and necessary habit, but in mime it is possible and essential to control it for the sake of preserving the dramatic line.

When I perform, I can feel my eyes react to the thought or mood of the character. Their muscles in their tensions and relaxations affect my face, as do the movements of my eyelids. Although I do not precalculate my eye reaction, when it does happen I am conscious of it, for it is as if there had been a break in the rhythmic line of the thought. Since I know that I cannot go long without blinking, I have come to develop a habit — by now quite automatic — of blinking between thought-phrases or while changing the direction of a glance. I use blinking, as a matter of fact, much as a writer uses a comma or period — as a punctuation mark.

*Seeing* is not only a matter of vision; it also has to do with understanding what one sees. The characters of the theatre, as human beings, must communicate through their eyes as well as through words. Much more intimately, in fact.

Gave the group exercises to make them aware of the feel of the eyes and lids: Had them first blink rapidly many times to relax the muscles; then, beginning with eyes lowered, slowly raise them, not permitting the lids to jerk but making them roll up smoothly instead; then, again slowly, lower them and blink at the end to release the tension.

Their eyes watered from the unaccustomed strain, and they confessed that their lids had jerked. After repeating this several times, their lids moved more smoothly and the watering ceased. Had them then roll their eyes one way, then blink and reverse the movement. Had them look about the room, quickly, at definite objects, blinking with each change of direction. Had them look slowly right, blink, return their gaze front, blink, and repeat the same left. At the end of this, not only were their eyes more relaxed and alive, but their faces were less tense.

Had them contract the upper muscles of their cheek bones and showed them, by example, how this might serve to narrow the eyes, particularly in Oriental roles — the example fascinated them.

Told them that this was something I had learned for myself when, before I had any idea of going into the theatre, I had become involved by accident in studying and performing for a brief period with two professional Japanese dancers. It is a very long time since then; but now, as I write of it, I find that these dances remain vivid in my senses, including what happened to my face and eyes while performing; like a remembered melody.

## Aside: The Seemingly Accidental

*Journal Note — December 1962*

A long-delayed first meeting with Marc Blitzstein took place at Irene and Aaron Diamond's, a meeting to which we had both looked forward but that had been prevented by our separate schedules.

He spoke of having first attended my performances in the early thirties when he was at work, under a W.P.A. grant, on the score for "The Cradle Will Rock," the show which brought him fame.

He said, hesitantly, that he hoped not to offend me by saying that he had enjoyed the performances as a kind of heightened vaudeville for he had expected to see another dance recital and had come only because of something he had read about what I did but which he could not exactly envision.

Assured him that, far from being hurt, I felt complimented by the association. This pleased him and we went on to find that we shared a mutual admiration for some of those great performers.

He seemed to wish to clarify his linking of what I do with vaudeville by telling that what had been a pleasant surprise was the unexpected variations in content and style of each number, so that satisfaction with each led into anticipation of the surprise to follow.

I was, of course, touched, but wishing to turn the direction of our conversation away from myself into another channel, replied that perhaps one reason for his surprise was due to there being no apparent over-all technical style in my performances as I had a predilection for the seemingly accidental.

This remark was badly chosen, for he was perplexed and took it as a championing of a current academic trend in the arts, the products of which he abhorred, which believes that anything goes that is achieved accidentally.

Nothing could have been further from my meaning but, to my dismay there was no time to explain, as we were parted by invading guests who protested our isolation.

Now, at home, the thought-train rattles on to its destination. I now realize that the word "seemingly" escaped him in the surrounding racket of voices. What I meant was the ability of a performer to arouse in the viewer a sense of being present at the moment of creation — that wonderful and intimate moment when we, as audience, feel that we are witnessing something which has never happened before nor will again.

It is in this art of the "seemingly accidental" that the great mimes of vaudeville were supreme. So were the best motion picture comics, but they had the advantage of having their best moments captured on film. Therefore, except for those who came from the stage, we cannot judge their abilities for repetitive performances.

## Vaudeville

No matter how often one saw these performers and thought that one remembered their "acts," one always experienced a wonderful pleasure of being taken unaware even in anticipated moments.

95

How did they accomplish this so that I, who would return after an interval to see my favorites repeat their memorable moments, was always delighted with recurrent surprise when these took place? Vivid as were their "acts" in memory, each time seemed a fresh improvisation although actually there was rarely any change.

I do not recall often experiencing this involuntary reaction at a second viewing of a play. There more often, my mind, against my will, wanders into side reflections; I become distracted by signs of technical devices and by personal idiosyncracies of the performer as apart from his character.

Vaudevillians had one important advantage over performers on the dramatic stage in that they created and performed their own characters. They had no director to whose interpretation of the play they had to conform. This is not to deny the importance of the director, but only to say that it is more difficult to bring an imposed image of a character to life than one invented by the performer himself. It is true that those vaudevillians who spoke often had outside writers, but the reading and performance of these lines were individual to the performer.

The success of the vaudevillian was established by the immediate response of the public at each performance. Vaudevillians faced in countless towns and cities the gruelling economic hazard of summary dismissal by a dissatisfied manager if the act failed. Nevertheless, despite economic discomforts, this brutal conditioning gave them opportunity to strengthen their acts through experimentation. They were again freer than dramatic actors in that they could work without fear of disastrous reprisals from a metropolitan critical press, which considered vaudeville, like burlesque, the lowest form of popular entertainment, unworthy of serious critical writing. Engagements at the Palace in New York, the ultimate to which any vaudevillian could aspire, never received detailed coverage in the press. It was only about the time of my own debut in the theatre, after some perceptive producers elevated vaudeville's most noted performers into the province of the Broadway revue and musical comedy, that they came to be written about as contributors to the "legitimate" theatre.

The first writers to do so were younger men, who also wrote about the achievements of the mimes in motion pictures — and, to my good fortune, about my own heretical excursions into the realm of mime.

Luckily for me, this was a time when the critical press was ready and willing to receive what I was trying to do. So was the public. But it is interesting to note that the dance world, then floundering to escape from earlier traditions, was the last to accept my departures. I was accused by their principal spokesman of not being a dancer — something which I never claimed — of being too "literary," too "theatrical," too esoteric or special, too anything which had no connection with the exalted ideals of "The Dance." That art, according to its principal exponents, could be ideally performed only in a cathedral. For my first performance I could find no title for what I did in mime, and as a convenient description I had labelled my creatures on the first programs as "compositions in dance form" — as one might say a composition in the form of a sonnet or sonata or short story. It was a critic dissatisfied with this phrase who coined "dance-mime," which subsequently became common to dance vocabulary. I myself, to dissociate myself from any idea that I was a dancer in the then conventional sense, chose to refer to what I did simply as "the theatre of A.E." so as not to be restricted to any set form for expressing the ideas which occurred to me. It was not until a few years later that

97

dancers, in search of a wider audience, became less restrictive and more generally theatrical in their approach.

But to return to thoughts of vaudeville: the vaudevillians through experience became philosophic, recognizing that public response was simply unpredictable, and thus hardened, perfected their work. Their practice studio was the stage, and through the responses of the audience they found a path to communicate their thoughts with instant effect. This contact with the audience, once made, was retained in memory, although the contact was not always established in the same way. They learned not only how to react to the nuances of thought of their stage characters, but how to project this in the right psychological instant to each audience, fully cognizant that each audience is a separate entity, and that no two are alike.

They worked as do night club performers today, many of whom have had this rigorous training; much in the manner, it seems to me logical to assume, as have all popular performers stemming from even preclassical days, a manner which grew into the form of the Commedia dell'Arte. It is, I believe, not unreasonable to assume that there were never more than a very few players in any age or in any form who were more than adequate. But the best contributed to the classic line of the theatre. We know that Molière was influenced in his dramatic form by them.

In my own case, like all the public of vaudeville, I was entranced by much that I saw. But I did not relate it to the ferment in my mind. Then, I probably would never have comprehended any influence, for I thouht of myself as working in isolation, working *against* what I had seen in the theatre and in dance.

But now, looking back, and pondering the recent discussion with Blitzstein, I conclude that I must have absorbed more

98

in dramatic expression from those players, particularly in projection, than I was conscious of.

## Aside: Timing and Counterpoint

Recently at a play, my attention was drawn to a lovely young actress as she made her entrance with admirable carriage, her arms hanging relaxed at her side, much in the manner of a species of goldfish in which the fins drag immobile as it floats — a not unattractive image of complete relaxation.

As she began to swim into intercourse with others in the scene, her discomfiture with the problem of using her hands and arms, in what should have been an unobtrusive, natural movement, was apparent.

It is a difficulty that young dancers often have in making the transference from habits of dance into acting in plays. That very training which perfects them in stylized dance forms hinders their walking and gestures in acting.

During the intermission I read of her experience in the program and found, as I suspected, that she was the product of a noted dance school whose director, I had once read, ventured the theory that the hands, as the last appendages of the body, are of least importance in expression.

This hypothesis is no doubt reasonable in those forms of dance concerned with exposition of an idea in terms of a technical pattern whereby the hands define the end of a designed movement executed in what has been referred to by one dancer, redundantly, as "empty space."

In mime, even in stylized forms as in the Oriental theatre, the hands do not serve as the ornamental finials of a designed

99

movement. Like the eyes and lips, and the feet as well, they are the ultimate physical points from which the meanings of the body and mind are projected in a kind of telegraphic code — no matter how unobtrusive or relaxed they may be.

In mime, a gesture, the end of the thought of a character, does not halt at the finger tips, for the message continues to communicate to the audience by way of the electrified atmosphere between them.

Every performer certain of his character knows that this sense of transmission has a dual effect and that the audience is a sounding board which throws back to him the information which it has received, confirming whether or not the intention of the character has reached its goal.

It is this, in part, with which timing is concerned. TIMING IS THE RHYTHM BETWEEN THOUGHT AND ACTION TO MAKE A POINT.

As a member of an audience I am rarely as carried away by calculated histrionics or by technical feats as I am by those fleeting nuances of expression, relayed by the extremities — hands, feet, eyes and lips — whereby the vagaries of the intimate reactions of a character are revealed. Reactions of which the character is unconscious but of which the performer as his intermediary is aware.

Without a musical sense of the relationship of the performer and his character, such nuances are not projected, for they are the result of a kind of jam session in which the performer acts as the conductor controlling the interrelated exchanges and responses of the thoughts and emotions of the character within a composite whole.

Samuel Butler wrote: "Sincerity is the lowest form of virtue." One might well apply this broad statement to mime wherein the performer must free himself, as much as is humanly possible, from his own libido as this can only succeed in making his characters earthbound to himself, denying them room for their own fancies.

Were I to recommend a basic course toward study of movement for a player who wishes to work freely, without sign of an imposed style of movement, it would be to play tennis or any racket or ball sport; to study music or to take lessons in tap and soft shoe dancing. These would imbue him with a sense of counterpoint and timing and would make nimble not only his hands and feet, but more importantly, his wits. It would, I believe, ingrain an acute sensitivity to variations in responses beyond those of set personal habits and prepare him to tackle problems in movement inevitable to the performer. To judge the direction and speed of a ball which must be hit and returned seems to me a more valuable exercise, dramatically speaking, so far as timing is concerned, than conventional dance training although I do not deny the latter's virtue in acquainting the body with general principles of movement.

The best tap and soft shoe dancers are marvelous in contrapuntal rhythm, for they can speak, gesture, deal with properties, all without breaking the complicated rhythm of their steps. As in tennis, their unified movements are breathtaking to behold.

A few years ago at a party I met George Abbott, the noted director who had begun in the theatre as a tap and soft shoe dancer, and I told of having been invited by Elliot Nugent, the actor-director, himself a former tap dancer, to watch him direct a scene on a Hollywood film stage. Nugent related how the scene had not progressed, as one of the players, not a beginner, could not cross the set, sit down, and reply, in one unbroken dramatic line, and thereby lost the timing of the key psychological moment. Nugent had performed it for him over and over again, making it come to life at each repetition, but to no avail, until at last he sighed and let the "take" pass.

Abbott shook his head sadly, and broodingly spoke about the lack of a sense of timing of the players in a play he was currently directing. Having in me a sympathetic audience, he jumped to his feet and performed a scene, not unlike Nugent's, in which he too was having difficulty with an actor. Instead of speaking, he accompanied his action by sounding the beat between his teeth against which he performed in counterpoint. What was remarkable was that although the scene could have been set down musically, that is, in contrapuntal movement against a beat, it appeared a natural, unstudied, improvisation. It had that dramatic suspense necessary to any performance which contrapuntal timing is instrumental in supplying. His body worked to the limits of its extremities, its entire nervous system uniting the wires of its life line to send off a single, comprehensible message to me, the enchanted viewer.

## Log: Fourteenth Session

### Tensions

Began today with a straight run-through of the play, mainly for my benefit, so that I might see whether or not the separate factors to be considered in the practice of mime and on which we have been dwelling, have converged with visible effect, as I have hoped.

Yes — somewhat: They move better — more freely and cleanly — they are less obstructed and cluttered by uncertainties and personal mannerisms. Also, happily, their performance does not appear calculated, and I could see that

102

my warnings "Careful, your technique is showing!" have been salutary.

However, they lack those shadings required in outlining individuality, for they are either intense or relaxed, without visible transitions between these two poles. They were puzzled when told this and several explained their state of thought in different instances — thoughts which they had *not* conveyed to me as viewer.

Told them that in mime it is insufficient to only *think*, for the audience is not a mind reader; and that thoughts must be telegraphed to the audience by actions — actions more sensed than seen — actions which are the automatic *reactions* to a thought or mood: an almost imperceptible sigh, a sudden intake of breath in coming to a decision, an effect on the lips of something seen — the unconscious responses natural to everyone which, flowing freely from thought, when we are oblivious of being observed, affect the reflexes of the nervous system. The importance to us of any thought or feeling is reflected in the nervous tensions of the body in natural behavior.

One might say that every human being has a life line — a fine wire attuned to receive and send forth the play of his thoughts. The tensile strength of this wire varies in each person and controls the outward expression of his thought-mood, even that which he may try to conceal (repression, too, is revelatory).

We say that a person is stolid or volatile, sensitive or insensitive, stupid or intelligent, etc. according to the way we see him react to this thought-mood — by the tensions and relaxations of his face and body, which also reveal the infinitesimal degrees of joy or terror, pleasure or pain — an entire state of being.

The mime needs to be as sensitive to the responses of his nerves to his thoughts as is a pianist to the responses of his

103

fingers to the keyboard. Tones of meaning in mime must be gauged and struck.

The novelist and poet inform us of their meaning through written description, narration, and the interplay of words and images, but in mime meaning can be revealed only by actual illustration. The mime must be tactilely susceptible to the scale of his tensile powers, which determine the pitch of his thought-mood.

This, at one and the same time, must be both instructive and controlled, in order that a performance can be repeated at will and still retain the essential quality of appearing to be improvised on the spur of the moment, even in highly stylized theatre forms. It is this tensile elasticity which not only colors and shades our meanings but which also keeps each performance fresh.

(It may be well to repeat that all theatre is stylized, that any performance or play is a designed composition, and that one of the problems in "naturalistic" acting is to conceal this.)

It is through bodily tensions that dramatic suspense is achieved technically. Thinking on it now in retrospect, I believe that the habit of performing some exercises in as slow and continuous a movement as possible, which I had always thought of simply in terms of control, was among the factors instrumental in building whatever time-sense I possess, for it taught me to apportion tensions of the body or to release them at will; to expend only the amount of energy required by the dramatic moment. It was a habit which became instinctive and which, I can see now, was invaluable in giving the characters which I perform what I can only call leisure to work in their own free way. I do not feel constricted by any urgent sense of time when I perform, even when the character is in a rush, for the composition takes into account the tensile

104

strength or life line of the character. That is, its thought-mood and nervous tensions work together.

The exercises which were given them today were designed to make them aware of extent of their utmost endurable state of tension, a state to be arrived at within a given span of time, which I set at three minutes.

Had them first sit, relaxed in a chair, eyes closed, breathing naturally, and concentrating on that length of time which I, watch in hand, called off. They were asked not to try to count off the seconds but to judge the time intuitively and open their eyes when they thought the three minutes were up.

Most of them opened their eyes long before the three minute mark, but two came fairly close. Admittedly this was not an easy exercise, but it gave me an indication of their time-sense, which, I believe, can be improved by practice.

Next, while retaining this time interval in memory, and beginning from a completely relaxed position in their chairs, lungs emptied, they were asked to become gradually tense, allowing their breathing to come as it had to, until at the end, a state of tension had been reached which would bring them up from their chairs and into a state of collapse. I called off only the starting and finishing points. The duration seemed to most of them an eternity, and they reached the acme of endurance long before the time was up, except, again, in two cases. But even these were less near the time mark.

One reason why they had not been able to sustain the suspense was that they had forgotten to take into account the accelerated rhythm of their breathing. Told them that I had not mentioned this contingency, as they had been expected to apply what they had been told about breathing some sessions ago.

After they had recovered from this strain, had them quickly recover their height of tension and from it slowly relax, as though in a faint or in a state of death.

As is usual after any of our exercises, most of which require concentration and cannot help but create tension, they fell into a spell of yawning, for they are unaccustomed to the rigors of sustained actions and thought.

We now improvised exercises in degrees of tension, the first of which I suggested as an experience common to all of them — waiting for an important telephone call, say that which would inform them whether or not they had been successful in reading for a part. They could do as they pleased while waiting, so long as their suspense built. Some chose to walk about, some to read, some to smoke, and some to just sit — but the tension was to be built and sustained until they heard the message and then released into happiness or melancholy.

There was no time limit for this as I "Br-r-r'd" whenever I saw it was least expected. They were asked to remember what they did — felt — so that it could be repeated with authenticity. What we found especially interesting in later discussion was how each one answered the telephone — the anticipation, eagerness, fear, indifference induced by hopelessness, and so forth.

After this they made up their own short scenes — quarrelled with each other, surprised each other, listened to incredible tall tales, walked in haste to witness an accident, watched a man being run over, screamed suddenly — anything that they could think of as practice in getting their sluggish nerves to react.

As we were finishing, I saw on the floor at my feet a pin, which, unthinkingly, I picked up. But feeling it between my fingers gave me a wicked idea. As I passed among them, saying that I had to make a telephone call in the lobby, I suddenly jabbed one of the men with the pin. He winced, froze, and, controlling himself, turned his head slowly and looked at me with surprise and a constrained smile of bewilderment. I admitted to the intention of outraging him, and asked him to immediately recall in detail what had happened — the electric effect of the prick and the chain of reactions which followed. I had to make an explanation to the others, who were mystified as to what had happened.

He took it with good grace, as I expected, for it is one of

106

the endearing qualities of this group that they accept me as a collaborator rather than a martinet imposing strict formulae on them.

In a way, the discipline which I exact from them is more demanding than they are aware, for its effects are insidious and each thing they learn seems to them to have been their own discovery. Which is the way I wish it to be, for I am unwilling to produce a group of automatons.

## Log: Fifteenth Session

Still not satisfied with their faces — particularly the sensitivity of their mouths, although there has been improvement. Occurred to me that one of the factors is the way they speak — the way most of us Americans do, from the throat, without sensing the formation of the sounds which make the words — the touch of the tongue against the teeth, or the shape of consonants felt by the lips. Their lips are more or less stationary as they speak, opened just enough to emit the sound. Of course one would not wish their lip and tongue action to be exaggerated, but practice would at least help them to clarify their final consonants and to project their words more clearly.

Thought to kill two birds with the same stone by giving them words to speak clearly, particularly noting those deplorably neglected final consonants. This drill would at the same time improve their articulation and exercise their tongues and lips, and so be of advantage to them both as mimes and as actors. Such an exercise would also provide a combination of speech and movement, useful to them since they intend making the spoken theatre their profession.

How to begin what is a new venture for me!

I am not good at devising technical exercises that are not directed toward some specific dramatic purpose. In trying to

107

devise something toward this end, remembered the preciseness
of cultivated French speech, which takes place largely between
the tip of the tongue and the lips. Remembered a few lines of
Verlaine upon which Debussy had based his "Fantoches,"
which I had once used as background music for a number:

Scaramouche et Pulcinella
Qu'un mauvais dessein rassembla,
Gesticulent, noirs sur la lune.

Here were words which required dramatic shadings and
rhythms as well as clear enunciation.

They were delighted at the idea. I wrote the lines on the
blackboard and they repeated them slowly after me, with
particular notice of the effect of each word on the tip of the
tongue and on the lips. After they had memorized the passage
had them say it several times with and without audible
sound, and as though in a whisper.

Then gave them a few lines from *The Merchant of Venice*
— where Portia, entering with Nerissa, says to her:

That light we see burning is in my hall.
How far that little candle throws his beams!
So shines a good deed in a naughty world.

This scene they were asked to enact with speech and gesture. It
entailed a number of problems in addition to the projection
of the words, whose rhythmic line was determined: first
the unexpected catching of Portia's eye by the candle, then her
comment on its brightness, and finally the resolution of this
into her philosophic comment. All this, for the purpose of the
exercise, to be performed with gesture — although as I pointed
out, it was not unlikely that a director of the play might
prefer no gestures at all. They must be prepared to adapt
themselves to any direction, but our purpose was to make them
feel at home with gesture.

Their enactment of the scene revealed that they were still
uncertain in gesture. What happened was a few indecisive
flounderings of the arms, raised and lowered without purpose
and without an eye to dramatic unity.

108

Quoted to them: "Nor do not saw the air too much with your hand, thus . . . I had as lief the town-crier spoke my lines."

Hamlet's speech to the players is only partly one which he himself would have thought of. That is, it is not strictly in character and within the plot line. It seems not unlikely to me that Shakespeare could not resist writing the concise and witty instructions — in which can be read his own struggles, as director, with the players in his company.

To return: After each one had performed the scene, both as Portia and as Nerissa (the men, out of context, as a man and a companion), we did as is customary with any dramatic exercise. We pulled it apart and put it back together again *after* we had made our mistakes.

In this case, all had made the same errors: First they had anticipated the direction from which the light would come, which took from their eyes the surprise of discovery. Also, their eyes did not focus on the imaginary light once it was found. (Suspense, however minute!) Discovery and focus on the light would have given an impetus for the first line:

"That light we see burning is in my hall."

Because of this hazy beginning, there was nothing in their faces and eyes to reflect the next wondering thought:

"How far that little candle throws his beams!"

the tone of which should have changed to a philosophic and witty note on the line:

"So shines a good deed in a naughty world."

The lines were read on a uniform tone level, although the diction had improved.

As to their gesture: Indication of the light had been vague, without rhythmic connection to the thought or the position of the light. Their arms had dropped helplessly at their sides at the end of each line and then risen again for the succeeding line, but with no effect.

Demonstrated how they had performed it, and they recognized how ineffectual their gestures had been.

Gave them an illustration of how one continuous gesture

containing some variety, could suffice. It went something like this:

"That light we see burning is in my hall."

*(The eyes were conscious of a light, the head turned, and the eyes had found its location. Read the line naturally, without undue emphasis but not from the back of the mouth, so that it is crystal clear. The arm raises easily, but not stretched full length, to point out the light. All relaxed, it points exactly in the direction of the gaze.)*

"How far that little candle throws his beams!"

*(A light note of wonder in the tone. Head and gaze unchanged; arm extends to its full length, and on the word "far" the fingers might spread as if to ray out into the distance.)*

"So shines a good deed in a naughty world."

*(Head turns to look at Nerissa; tone casually philosophic; arm brought back, fingers relaxing; palm turned upward with a slight accent on the word "so," is held through "shines a good deed," and drops naturally to the side during the remainder of the line, timed so that it is in place by the final consonant of "world.")*

Explained that, in a play, no gesture must detract from the spoken word. That if a descriptive gesture is used at all, its passage must be simple and direct and must draw a picture in the eyes of the audience *only to enhance the words*. It must be the natural expression of the word or thought-mood. In some plays, a character may have nervous mannerisms, but even these must be carefully considered and used only at planned points. The arms and hands cannot flail about distracting the viewer from listening, and where there are no words and the meaning of a thought-mood is dependent on

110

gestures, these not only must be descriptive, but must be in rhythmic harmony with the entire intent of the body and mind. The gesture is the ultimate nervous reaction of these.

Each performed the scene again, with marked improvement, in the eyes of us who watched.

Ran even longer than usual overtime, and two of the players asked if I would help them with scenes they were preparing for another class. Agreed to come a half hour earlier for this.

## Log: Sixteenth Session

Came earlier, as promised, and found that a number of the other players had turned up ahead of time to watch. Worked mostly on an Ibsen scene, whose problems in the combination of words, movement, style, etc. I found so engrossing that the regular session of our class was late in starting.

Had come prepared with a project of mime combined with words, to be performed with a musical background — all planned to give them practice in sustained mood. For this, made a quick and not very good translation of a Verlaine poem, "Colloque Sentimental" (they withdraw from romantic sentiment).

This is it: to be performed by two characters, an elderly man and woman who have been lovers, who meet unexpectedly in a park, and for a few moments try to recall their former life together. The descriptive verses to be read by a stranger, who stands at the far side of the stage — a compère. A piece by Fauré, which I played them, sets the background mood.

### Colloque Sentimental

COMPÈRE   In the deserted park, silent and vast
           Erewhile two shadows, glimmering figures, passed.
           Their lips were colorless, and dead their eyes;

111

|          | Their words were scarce more audible than sighs. |
|----------|--------------------------------------------------|

Their words were scarce more audible than sighs.
In the deserted park, silent and vast
Two spectres conjured up the buried past.

HE: Our ancient ecstasy, do you recall?

SHE: Why, pray, should I remember it at all?

HE: Does your heart at mention of me glow?
Do you still join our lips in slumber?

SHE: No.

HE: Ah, blessed, blissful days when our lips met.
You loved me so!

SHE: Quite likely, I forget.

HE: How sweet was hope, the sky how blue and fair!

SHE: The sky grew black, the hope became despair.

COMPÈRE: Thus they walked 'mid the frozen weeds, these dead,
And night alone o'erheard the things they said.

The rhythm of the lines was set by practice, and everything they did contrapuntally had to be resolved to fall within the beat.

Particular words were practiced for color — so that the word "vast" communicated a feeling of space; the word "dead" had a flat finality; the word "frozen" had to be cold and congealed; and so on. All the movements of the pair were to give a sense of the period of Verlaine and also a feeling of melancholy, so that the audience would see the park, through their movements and voices, as deserted and bathed in a mist. The whole to project a macabre aspect, the pair, an air of elegance.

The entire scene to have a mesmeric effect on the viewer.

While they were not successful in establishing the atmospheric whole as I had envisioned it, and seemed ill at ease with what was demanded from them, I myself was entranced with the idea. In my imagination its aroma was enormously provocative, for in flavor alone it was not unlike a few of my own theatre pieces, done without words. I tried to show the women how I thought it might be done, but found

112

that they could not transmigrate themselves into the style of another age.

## Log: Seventeenth Session

Today brought yards of fabrics of different textures from home, and these, together with draperies from the property room, we fashioned into a variety of robes, tunics, scarves, etc. The purpose was to experience the effects of gesture and movement on draperies of different sorts. We walked, turned, sat, rose and turned, ran, knelt, and so on.

Suggested that we practice entering a room, bowing and curtseying in period styles; and learned at this late date that their one or two years of dramatic training had not informed them of these essentials! Showed them how to take off and put on hats of different periods. Lectured them on not having had the intelligence to search in the public library, where such information could be found. This gave me an opportunity to inquire whether, as I had suggested early in our meetings, they had read literature of other periods in which they could discover the modes and manners of different societies, as well as the thought, all of which could stimulate their imaginations. Only one, a beginner, had had "time" ( which I translated as sufficient interest) for this, and it had been apparent in his work. For once, stopped the class on the minute and, refusing to answer questions, left immediately.

## Log: Eighteenth Session

Today an exercise to be performed in the styles of the seventeenth, eighteenth, and nineteenth centuries, which also

113

provided the men practice in forms of greeting and use of (improvised) hats.

Romantic in mood, performed with and without comic overtones and with and without a few words.

## Plot

A young woman is seated next to a small table, LEFT — HALF UP. She is embroidering, and her mood is unhappy and slightly petulant.

Her maid and confidante enters UP CENTER, bringing a note; on opening it, she discovers with a resigned sigh that it is from her lover, with whom she has quarrelled.

The maid, accustomed to a degree of familiarity with her mistress, tries to read it over her shoulder but is motioned away.

The letter is read. It asks forgiveness, but this requires reflection. The maid indicates that the lover is waiting outside, and the woman decides to permit him to enter. She resumes her needlework, which she continues while he enters and beseeches her to relent. She refuses. In despair, he walks dramatically to the opposite side of the room, stands for a moment, then turns to look at her. She looks at him, he holds out his arms; after a moment of hesitation, she relents, puts aside her embroidery, and rushes into his arms.

This was no easy, frivolous exercise, for it contained a number of technical problems: the relationship between the maid and her mistress; the maid's automatic short curtsey; the way the embroidery was to be placed on the table and how the young woman was to rise and turn, as though full-skirted; the line of her figure as she rushed forward; the way he caught her and held her; and the way she relaxed into his arms and placed her head on his shoulder. All to be done with suspense, to be romantically touching, or else to contain a degree of humor.

114

I had to demonstrate each character several times; for as has been noted before, it is easy for these players to be extremely dramatic in their movements but difficult for them to sustain the mood of romantic comedy. But they are much freer now than when we began.

The art of mime requires retaining a line of suspense while performing seemingly inconsequential actions.

## Log: Nineteenth Session

Relented and came an hour early to help several of them to block scenes which they are preparing for tryouts for summer stock.

Went over what we had worked on these past weeks, and went through mime-play — a stop-go — considering the possible applications of the exercises. Ran overtime because we went into rehearsal of other dramatic sequences. The players were gratified at being heartily applauded by an audience of the next class, which had come early to watch.

## Log: Twentieth Session

### Recapitulation

Our last session, although they assume that shortly we will resume work. I am not yet decided, for too much time is spent between meetings thinking of solutions to their problems, to the neglect of my own!

The failure to bring the play to fruition was due to the limited time in which we had to work. We all recognized that we had been too optimistic about the undertaking. I do not feel badly that it was not completed, for it was conceived

115

solely as a device for unified study of many characters. The truth is that I do not believe that mime performed by large groups is interesting dramatically unless augmented by sounds or words. It is a highly intimate medium of expression and its essence is lost when performed en masse. Even in the classic Commedia dell'Arte, sounds and words were incorporated.

What had become immediately apparent was that the group felt helplessly stranded in a fearsome foreign territory without an adequate sign language with which to communicate; they had expected to learn an alphabet from me, but they didn't.

They awakened to learn that what I did in the theatre was not accomplished by such simple means as it had appeared to them in watching my performances. At the same time I had been equally taken aback that their former training had not prepared them to receive what I had to offer, which was detailed examination of ways of evolving character, ways to achieve those subtle transitions in actions and mood upon which all quality in such revelation depends. They had formed the habit of accepting the director's interpretation of a character, and were at a loss as to how to use the freedom that I gave them.

Their points of view were further myopic in that while they had a wide acquaintance with plays, they were ignorant of the times and places from which the plays emerged. Thus, they regarded the characters of playwrights as figures isolated from their eras and societies in which they moved. They had, I was astonished to find, a far more parochial view toward what they saw, read, or heard than I had had at their age. They could not transcend their own experiences; they could not make themselves truly compatible with unfamiliar points of view.

For this reason, much time had to be spent talking to them in an endeavor to widen their perspectives. In this I think I had some success, although I know that in a few instances such diversions were resented by those impatient to be given an easily applied rote formula.

All in all I found the term an enlightening experience and

am inclined to continue for a purely selfish reason. I have come to love them all dearly, for in each one I find symptoms of the complex problems I confront in my own work. To me they are not pupils to be handed set rules, they are extensions of myself in constant search.

I had hoped that several would emerge not as rubber-stamp reproductions of myself but as performers who might offer their own fresh contributions.

Evaluating them according to what I first expected, I find that the three beginners have proved more free, inventively, than those with dramatic training. These latter have been overly bound by an inclination to tie the impulses of their characters too literally to their own personal responses. This not only has hindered their improvisations (except those directly related to themselves as the characters) but has made the transitional moments of justification obvious, as I tried to point out earlier. Of the two dancers, the girl, after overcoming the shock of not being given a technical pattern to learn, has done fairly well, considering that she is not accustomed to thinking beyond technical exercises and has never quite rid herself of the mannerisms of her former training. The other dancer, a man from whom I at first did not expect much, has done very well; for, like the three beginners, he has not been afraid of his imaginings.

The most experienced group have had what seemed to me another handicap. In their greater knowledge of plays and players, they would search their memories for ideas and were mystified as to why I found the fresh inventions of the beginners more interesting than those presented by them. Because of their inclination to draw upon their memory of performances seen and admired, I chose to end our season by speaking about *style*.

Style is an abstract word of shaded meanings. It is that quality in a person which reveals his singularity and in this context is synonymous with manner.

In the arts, style is more complex, as it entails the expression of a point of view resolved through technique. In the best sense, style is not a cloak put on for outward show, like a fashionable or exotic dress, but is something which evolves in the process of finding the best possible way of recording what one has to say.

In learning his craft it is not unusual for the beginning artist to try to emulate the style of someone whose work he admires. But by continuation of this imitative line, more often than not his work recalls to the perceptive viewer the virtues of its source and obscures the individuality of the novice.

In the act of living everyone is influenced by direct experience or by learning what has been done and thought by others beyond immediate, personal contact; for human beings do not exist in a vacuum. It is this learning, combined with the development of personal preferences and standards of taste, which along with solving technical difficulties is instrumental in forming a personal style in the arts.

I do not believe that those artists whose works we now regard as classics of their genre were concerned with setting down a definitive recognizable style, a fashion of working, for this would have limited their ultimate growth, both in perception and technique.

We see this best in painting, where what we come to call the ultimate style of a painter is the apotheosis of what he has to say by whatever technical means he can muster in conjunction with his personal taste.

118

I doubt whether anyone who works in the arts is often satisfied with his style or accepts it as a constant. He does the best
he can within his capabilities at the moment, and whether or
not this is communicated to others as a personal point of view
is pure chance. Each work is a starting point for the next and
this leads him, by degrees, into finding a compatible way of
working which, eventually, to the outward eye, defines his
style. His ideal may be far removed from what he is able to
accomplish. For example, we see in the works of Picasso an
obsession with the art of the past and an attempt to recapture
the classic line of life, an attempt which, formed by his own
point of view, created his changing styles. But underneath these
changes there remains a portrait of his own individuality.

The player has not the advantage of the time given to writers, composers, and painters, for the seeds of his perception
must sprout into view at the first opportunity he has to appear
before the public. Moreover, he cannot *see* what he does and
can only judge his image by its effect on the audience.

But for the young player to assume that an initial enthusiastic reception is tantamount to his having a style can be more
a hindrance than an asset to his future work. The audience is
delighted at first at the appearance of a new figure and it can
also quickly weary of repetitive mannerisms unless these are
especially engaging, so much so that the role played is of minor
import.

Otherwise in the theatre, as in any of the arts, a contrived
style reveals more facility than perception in the player and is
a dead end in so far as the craft of performing may be considered an art whereby the executant of a character in any theatre
form can contribute the sum total of his understanding to the
best of his intuitive and technical knowledge. Together, these
will set his style, in conjunction with that *picture of the charac-*

119

*ter* which should be vivid in his mind if he is qualified to be a performer.


*Postscript to Style*

A style may also be the result of the conditions under which one is forced to work.

Juan Belmonte, the noted matador who established what became a classic precedent in bullfighting, became famous for his brave style of fighting close to the bull, so close, as I witnessed, that the bull often brushed his body in passing. In a book Belmonte tells how this style developed through necessity. As a young boy from the poorest quarter of Seville, he was determined to become a bullfighter. The only way he could get training was to steal out on moonlit nights into the pastures where fighting bulls were at large. There, because of the light, it was impossible to gauge and anticipate their movements except at close range. In addition, he had to work cautiously for fear of causing a stampede, which would awaken the overseer. In this way he learned how to approach a bull without arousing it to violent action until he was very close and then how to feel and escape its sudden impulses. It is true, as anyone who saw him knows, that he worked so closely to the animal as to make it sometimes appear that they were adversaries interlocked in combat or were even one creature; a breathtaking spectacle and a style of fighting which influenced all subsequent matadors in their attempts to prove themselves equally brave.

Reading Belmonte's account of his early training, it struck me that we had one thing in common which had influenced our

120

separate styles. This was the circumstance under which we both had had to work in the beginning: the limitation of space.

Mine required no bravery but it did demand working within a confined area, that of the bedroom which was my living quarter. I could not afford to engage studio space and had to condition myself to imagine an extended area in which the characters could be more ideally performed. This meant sensing the possibilities of extension of their movements, much as a composer hears his music in performance as he sets it down.

The small, irregular area where I worked, broken by immovable furniture, was a training in control. Any decorative flights in movement extraneous to the character were impossible and all had to be pared to essentials. This had an indelible effect on the way in which I work and made adjustment in pacing on any stage easy. A sense of the composition of my concept was so firmly established that only repacing for timing was required to accommodate myself to any stage — which quickly became home.

I never thought of myself as having a recognizable style, for it had been among my primary purposes to escape an over-all form, letting each idea take its own form instead. Consequently I was surprised when I first read that I had an individual style. I remember that I tried, unsuccessfully, to envision what others were seeing as my style. I tried to fathom where some movement characteristic of me interfered with the characters as I saw them. Since I do not see myself, in imagination, as I perform, but see only the characters, I decided it was best to leave well enough alone rather than become distracted by viewing myself in a mirror as I performed, which I was certain would only be disruptive.

121

Over the years I have found it impossible to explain to others that I do not believe myself a natural performer in the sense that I do not play *to* an audience. Performing to me is never a projection of myself but a kind of sharing of ideas with others. I get the same enjoyment I have while evolving the characters, perhaps an enjoyment even more intense. That what I did happened to strike a sympathetic note to the audiences was purely accidental. Had it not been so I would have been as well content, despite the pressing economic hazards, to work privately as a painter and a writer.

But, as it happened, what I write or paint has to do with ideas which are impossible for me to perform myself because of the limits imposed by a single performer in the medium of mime.

## Aside: Programming

*Journal Note: January 3, 1963*

Spent most of day arranging and pasting up program copy, which Bureau wants immediately, for forthcoming performances. They are willing to relieve me of this tiresome chore, but I prefer to do it myself to make as certain as possible that the correct program, together with a list of its stage requirements, is received by the theatre for which it is designed.

I think of each program as one dramatic unit, just as is each separate number on it: I see the whole as a kind of fever chart, with gradual ups and downs of increasing intensity and demands for concentration from the audience, until the very end where it is released by some lighter number — something easily grasped and in a comic vein, and something not too foreign to their own experience.

Since my performances are in a personal mime form, each audience must from the start be led into viewing them with a fresh eye. But even in those places where I've appeared often, I find that the rule for the dramatic progression of the program *works* for me — although it may not for others, and it certainly cannot be applied to plays in quite the same manner.

The styles of the numbers vary: some are in a "natural" style, some more formal, some more obviously rhythmic, in the sense that dance is more obviously rhythmic than drama. Also, there are mood changes: some of the numbers are romantic, some satiric, others tragic, dramatic, or abstract presentations of one aspect of an age as represented through a character of its society.

But the entire program is carefully planned so that these diverse and sometimes seemingly erratic mood changes have a dramatic logic; for each number not only fulfills its own purpose but prepares the audience for the one which follows. Sometimes the mood is continued to a greater height; sometimes a number is placed so as to release an audience from the mood of the previous number and also to prepare it for the one to follow.

The plan of a program is based solely on my instinctive sense of what I, as a viewer, am prepared to receive.

As this stranger to myself-as-character, I begin on what I call a "slow note." Not necessarily slow in *speed*, but something easily and quickly assimilated by an audience uncertain as to the sort of thing they will see, as in my case they often are. I want to give the audience time to settle into acceptance of my particular form — and also, in this adjustment, to get

123

over the first shock of my actual appearance, in contrast to their preconceived image and, perhaps, hopes!

Every performer knows that this contingency always exists, no matter how concealing the makeup; there is always that moment of a first entrance in which the audience searches out the identity of the performer behind his character. It is a transition which takes place quickly, but I like to get it out of the way. I do so by permitting some seconds — regardless of the speed with which the character enters or his actions if he is "discovered" — for the audience to make this adjustment, but in a manner of which they are not aware; for I myself exist only as the character on rise of curtain. It is part of timing.

As the program progresses, I may juxtapose an acrid or satiric number against a romantic one, depending on what change in mood I feel the audience is ready for. The program contains one intermission, which for my purpose I have found better than two, as there were in my first performances. This is a personal predilection of mine, even at plays, where I find more than one intermission break tiresome, although I know that players may be delighted to have the respite.

In my case, the second half of the performance demands the greater concentration from the audience. The first half is a preparation in growing suspense for what is to follow.

It has been my experience, and managers have remarked on it, that the audience does not become restive during the periods of costume change. This, I think, is due to the planning of the dramatic line of the program, which, in addition to the increasing suspense of each number, includes as well the surprise of its pictorial aspect. It may be all these factors taken together that caused Marc Blitzstein to relate what I do to vaudeville.

Programming a solo performance presents many problems which the actor in plays is not called upon to solve, nor are those performers who appear with companies.

In undertaking to work with my student group, I had had a notion of finding players who could act as ties between one number and another in my own programs, and I had had ideas with which I longed to experiment. But this did not transpire. I've discussed the thought with a few persons but have found that they all believe it would inject an unwelcome foreign note into the dramatic line of the programs as they now stand.

## Aside: Mime is a Lonely Art

Mime is a lonely art, for the mime works in a solitary world inhabited by phantasms which take only transient physical form through him.

Anything extraneous to their will — such as an attempt by the mime to draw attention to himself by signals to the audience that he, like them, appreciates the foibles of his characters — causes these creatures to withdraw in a sulk, and the mime discovers himself stranded with only his own ego for company. At that moment when he feels obliged to step out of his character to communicate personally with the audience, he pays the heavy penalty of becoming estranged from the figures of his imagined world and of being forsaken by the audience.

I can illustrate this by an experience I once had. Some of my performances were given in rural communities where I was the first "live" performer the audience had seen except for a few instrumentalists and singers, not to mention local student productions of the then ubiquitous *Kiss and Tell,* an already passé Broadway hit.

At two consecutive such performances, the audience seemed perplexed at what I was doing until the second or third number. I thought I would try to gain a more immediate response by slight exaggerations of glances or movements, in an effort to communicate with the audience more quickly. While these actions aroused audible signs of life, I soon realized that they had nothing to do with understanding of the character, but were only taken as an indication to the audience that I was on their side rather than in sympathetic and sustained accord with the figure performed.

I remember distinctly saying to myself after the second try, while changing into the third costume, "After this I will mind my own business!"

This proved good advice; for I found out, from later comments, that what I had believed to be a failure of the audience to respond in the manner I expected was, in fact, only their concentration on what I was doing: they were enjoying a gradual awakening — a slow transference of their understanding from their own time and place to those which appeared so unexpectedly before their eyes. This was evidenced by their growing response to succeeding numbers. In that sense, audiences are not unlike visitors to a foreign land who discover that the modes, manners, and thought of its inhabitants are not meaningless oddities, but are sensible in context.

Mime opens up a new world to the beholder, but it does so insidiously, not by purposely injecting points of interest in the manner of a teacher or tour guide. The mime is no more than the physical medium — the instrument on which the fig-

*"Pique-Nique — Dejeuner au Bois, 1860"*

ures of his imagination play their dance of life. He, or she, is a lonely figure in whom neither the audience nor the figures of their imagination have any interest. As in any of the creative arts, the viewer is concerned only with the results of the invention.

To me, the realization of this loneliness is an asset, for it provides a sense of that isolation in which one is free to abandon oneself to the expression of those images with which one is obsessed.

But the audience for mime also has responsibilities – it must be an alert collaborator. It cannot sit back, mindlessly complacent, and wait to have its emotions titillated by mesmeric musical sounds or visual rhythms or acrobatic feats, or by words which tell it what to think. Mime is an art which, paradoxically, appeals both to those who go to a theatre or circus free to respond instinctively to whatever they see, and to those with sophisticated, whetted perceptions. Between these extremes lie those audiences conditioned to resist any collaboration with what is played before them; and these the mime must seduce despite themselves. There is only one way to attack those reluctant minds – take them unaware! They will be delighted at an unexpected pleasure.

## Aside: Before the Act

All the exigencies which arise in traveling, as I do, with no crew except an accompanist and sometimes a dresser, have, I believe, given profitable experience, however exhausting, which actors do not have. To each advance copy of the program is attached a list of my property and stage requirements, and I must take it on faith that these will be forthcoming. Only rarely does this happen; thus every performance, except when there is a run in the same theatre, is a first time. Actors, on tour or in New York runs, are relieved of any duties beyond playing their parts. When they arrive in a town, they are fairly sure to find sets and lights identical to what they are accustomed to working with.

Not so with me. It has become my habit, formed by necessity, to walk about the stage on first arrival at a theatre or auditorium where I am to perform within a few hours. There I get an intimation of the adjustments that must be made in timing and movement according to the ever changing space limits. I also make a quick calculation of the proportions of the space which will contain the audience, as this has strong bearing on the timing and projection required.

Next, I examine the lighting equipment at my disposal and confer with the head electrician. And I have my first look at the properties, which are only rarely completely assembled and are seldom what I optimistically hope to find.

It is my experience to be greeted by wary-eyed stage crews prepared to defend themselves against demands for the impossible. This situation requires considerable diplomacy in those cases where what is available is, at first sight, disappointing. It is true that I am a devil for detail; but, on the other hand, I learned early to make do with what is possible. To me any stage is home; and I take it for granted that its behind-the-scenes workers are close relatives, as interested as I am in making it a comfortable place in which to live for a few hours.

We then go into rehearsal, which consists of setting the lights and planning the placing and removal of the properties.

130

Since the stagehands are often unfamiliar with what I do, I myself write down the light and property plot, so that they know exactly what I expect. Lights are angled and changes of color noted, as are dimout and blackout cues. Sometimes I can suggest means of getting lighting effects never before attempted, but it is very rare — I can remember no specific instance — that a crew has been recalcitrant in its cooperation. In fact, it often happens that when we have not achieved a desired effect by the time I must go to makeup I am pleasantly surprised to find in a hasty check-up just before curtain that in some way they have managed, within that short time, to give me more than I had hoped for in lights and properties, or that a hand property which I have brought in a precarious state has been repaired, or that a chair has been regilded or reupholstered. I usually come away from a performance with a deep affection for the crew, even for the most hard-bitten professionals, although I well know that to all of them I am only another performer gotten out of the way.

## The Send-Off

And at last, fully cognizant of the hazards which lurk ahead, the moment comes to every performer when he must face the battery of eyes trained on him from the front; a moment in which he feels stranded in space; a moment when reason deserts him and he is at the mercy of feeling. It is then that he can only hope to be struck by the light of instinct, and call to it, as the vaudevillian Al Jolson, with a note of combined agony

131

and authority, did to the god manipulating the spotlight in a
topmost balcony, as if for benediction from a celestial symbol:

*Gimme the Moon!*

**CURTAIN**